Transforming Therapy through Horses

Transforming Therapy through Horses

CASE STORIES TEACHING THE EAGALA MODEL IN ACTION

**Lynn Thomas, LCSW
and Mark Lytle**

with Brenda Dammann

Transforming Therapy through Horses
Case Stories Teaching the EAGALA Model in Action

© 2016 by EAGALA, the Equine Assisted Growth and Learning Association

EAGALA
PO Box 993
Santaquin, UT 84655 USA
www.eagala.org
equine@eagala.org

Disclaimer
The information provided in this publication is for general informational purposes only. All activities involving horses have inherent risks, including dangers to life and limb. Any individuals or practitioners who wish to participate in equine-assisted psychotherapy should do so only under appropriate supervision and/or after receiving proper training. The authors and the Equine Assisted Growth and Learning Association (EAGALA) do not make any representations or warranties as to the information in this publication and expressly disclaim any and all liability arising out of participation in or utilization of any techniques, experiences, or activities involving horses.

ISBN: 1523239468
ISBN 13: 9781523239467

Contents

Disclaimer

The stories in this book come from actual EAGALA cases.
The identities of the clients have been changed to protect their privacy.

Acknowledgment

The Equine Assisted Growth and Learning Association (EAGALA) is grateful for the generous financial support of Frank and Nonie Reed, EAGALA practitioners and founders of Touchstone Ranch Recovery Center (touchstoneranchrecovery.com), in making this book possible.

Here's a bit of Frank's story in his own words:

I was introduced to the EAGALA Model in 2010 through my wife, Nonie. She became acquainted with the model after hearing about it at a horse show, and, after taking a look, she became excited about using horses in therapy. As a licensed chemical-dependency counselor, she could see the possibilities right away.

It took me a while longer. When I first heard about EAGALA from Nonie, my business mind immediately began thinking about how much money I could make buying and selling horses to EAGALA programs. But I was totally against using our show horses in sessions. "We're not using our horses—our expensive show and cutting horses—around these clients," I said. But Nonie was persistent, so I agreed to go take a look and see what this was all about. That's how I ended up at my first training.

The idea of selling horses quickly faded as I went through the training and saw things happen. I began to understand how EAGALA could help our clients at Touchstone Ranch recover from alcohol and drugs. So I started going to multiple trainings: several Part Ones and Part Twos and then Advanced Trainings and just about every other training EAGALA has. We brought the EAGALA Model home and started using it at our facility.

I've been doing this now since 2010, and I've seen several marvels take place. You can walk into a session and see the clients' dynamics change. While I was initially against putting my own show horses into EAGALA sessions with clients, I began seeing how the horses changed as well. As they interact with clients, I've watched miracle after miracle take place. These clients have no idea how much those horses are worth in the show ring, and it doesn't matter. All that matters is the healing.

It's unbelievable how EAGALA work has changed me as well. I've learned so much about myself being in there. The EAGALA Model makes you very clear about yourself. When I went to Advanced Training, I saw a lot of things that were still stuck inside of me come out. I got more personal development out of EAGALA training than I did out of anything else.

In early 1987, as a military veteran, I was so sick from drugs and alcohol I couldn't even get up off the floor. I'd start every day with a drink of whiskey and a needle in my arm. I finally became fed up and asked God for help. I haven't touched anything since. I rebuilt my life, became a successful businessman, and established Touchstone Ranch Recovery Center in the process.

Now I see so many clients changing their lives through the EAGALA Model. That's why Nonie and I sponsor EAGALA today and why I gladly sponsor the publishing of this book. We are 100 percent behind EAGALA and will do whatever we can to help it grow.

Introduction

I had been working in EAGALA Model equine-assisted psychotherapy for many years when "Julie" arrived as a new participant in our program's anger management group. As she was checking in, I asked, "What brings you down here to the barn and to this group?"

She said, "Well, this girl looked at my boyfriend, so I stabbed her in the neck with a fork."

My eyebrows lifted. "Oh! Well...welcome to anger management."

Julie was fourteen years old and had some significant struggles in life. She had been adopted at the age of two and was now a volatile teenager, prone to violent outbursts and extreme bouts of rage. She had a particularly terrible relationship with her parents and difficult relationships in general. She was resistant to everything. Individual therapy was not progressing well.

Initially her resistance also included working with the horses. It took some time for her to get into the groove of the group. Then she started to have some breakthroughs. We began to see that even though there were times when she struggled and would not participate, she always showed up. Her primary therapist began reporting that she was sharing what was happening at the barn in her individual therapy sessions.

Eventually Julie started making progress. She was consistently coming to the barn, and while she didn't warm up to us as facilitators, she *did* warm up to the horses. At one point I asked her, "What do you get out of working with the horses?"

She replied, "I can't have an attitude with the horses. When I have an attitude, they confront me. They get an attitude right back."

Julie became more and more successful in her sessions. She began to demonstrate leadership skills and develop stronger, more positive relationships. As Julie's progress continued, she was able to transition from the anger management group into our day-treatment program. Ultimately, she was able to return to traditional school.

When I reflect on this story, I am amazed at how far Julie came. Her journey is an example of the power of the horses and the EAGALA Model at work. The work we did provided the breakthrough that got her out of trouble and helped create significant changes in her family and community relationships.

What happened to create the breakthrough in this story? How did horses impact this client's transformation? What kind of process can lead to these significant outcomes?

This book will share this process and the training behind it. Through the powerful example of case stories, we will explore aspects of a therapeutic model incorporating the unique engagement of horses and the specialized skill sets of a human team interacting with the innate potential of our clients to find solutions.

Around the world, people from all walks of life—troubled teens to traumatized military vets to struggling families—are using the EAGALA Model of equine-assisted psychotherapy (EAP) to grapple with their issues. Arriving at horse barns and rural farmsteads, they enter open-air arenas to engage in this process. When they emerge, their perspective has shifted, and very often their lives have been placed on the road to change.

In this evolving field of mental health practice, which can also incorporate both personal and professional growth and learning modalities, horses are intentionally incorporated into the human therapeutic process and placed at the focal point of client sessions. The Equine Assisted Growth and Learning Association, known as EAGALA, evolved this model to harness the innate capacity of horses to influence people in incredible ways. The mental health component is called equine-assisted psychotherapy (EAP). The learning modality used for personal, professional, and corporate purposes is called equine-assisted learning (EAL).

EAGALA Model practice is unique in that the human counterparts of the treatment team take a backseat in client sessions. Horses are front and center, deliberately unhindered, and allowed to interact with clients as they wish. As EAGALA's training manual explains, EAP is different from traditional therapy in that it is "about the relationship between the horses and clients, *not* the relationship between the facilitators and clients. The facilitators are there to provide the opportunities and bring consciousness to the lessons being learned."[1]

This "hands-off" scenario creates the environment for change and, more often than not, opens doors to the unexpected and unplanned. As the process unfolds, the horses' impact on the client experience often takes surprising turns, creating amazing stories in the process.

---

1 EAGALA, *Fundamentals of the EAGALA Model, 8th Edition Training Manual* (Santaquin, UT: EAGALA, 2015), 15.

Though the EAGALA Model sounds quite simple, allowing the horse-client relationship to evolve unhindered is often more difficult in practice than it appears on paper. The two human members of the EAGALA therapeutic team—a licensed mental health practitioner and an equine specialist—often come from backgrounds steeped in traditional methods of training. For the treatment team, utilizing their formal training methods in a different way and leaving expectations behind require discipline and ongoing practice. Yet over and over again, the results are clear. When facilitators are skilled enough to remove their influence from the session, remarkable things happen for their clients.

Horses are nuanced creatures, and working with them in this capacity is a nuanced practice. New facilitators soon learn that the EAGALA principles, put into a single training manual, can take years to understand fully. As a facilitator's experience grows, core concepts reveal themselves in layers, coming to life in countless ways inside client sessions. It can take dozens—if not hundreds—of sessions, along with ongoing training and mentoring, to truly become skilled as facilitators. To work well, the EAGALA Model requires its practitioners to reach beyond their individual understanding and their comfort zones, to continually let go of expectations, and to be truly present to adapt and improvise in client sessions.

For those with a fascination for learning, equine-assisted practice becomes endlessly intriguing. As stories unfold in the arena, this model not only improves the lives of its clients but enriches the personal development of its practitioners as well.

The challenge for EAGALA leadership involves finding an effective way to ingrain these principles, which seem so basic at the outset, so that practitioners understand the full spectrum of complexity and develop the necessary presence of mind to enhance their clients' potential for growth, learning, and healing.

This is where our stories come in.

In 2011, EAGALA founder and CEO Lynn Thomas and EAGALA trainer Mark Lytle created a conference workshop to teach the core tenets of the EAGALA Model by utilizing Mark's natural storytelling talents. An EAGALA Model facilitator since 2001, Mark became a professional trainer for EAGALA in 2003, teaching professionals around the world. Stories from his own client cases quickly became the focal point of Mark's training. Mark collaborated with Lynn to present these same stories in a conference setting to illustrate facets of the EAGALA Model in action. The pair found this method effective in creating deeper dialogue around the EAGALA principles.

"Over the years practicing EAGALA, I've been blessed with challenging cases that make great learning stories," says Mark, with more than a little a touch of irony. "Through it all, Lynn has been a mentor, someone I could always reach out to in the process. I have devoted my life to this model. Even after years spent working and training as an EAGALA practitioner, I continue to learn. The root of most of my stories is me messing up and learning the lessons I need to become a better facilitator. But the stories are also about the way our horses have changed, how our clients have changed, and how I have changed as a practitioner."

According to one Native American proverb, "It takes a thousand voices to tell a single story." Experienced EAGALA facilitators soon learn it takes a thousand stories to truly appreciate the many ways horses can evoke positive change in human clients. Through the best stories from this EAGALA storytelling conference workshop—each modified to protect client confidentiality—this book will enable you to meet an amazing array of equine characters while also unraveling many facets of EAGALA practice: How do horses actually work in therapy settings? How do we "trust the process"? How can the facilitators learn from the art of improvisation?

For new and prospective EAGALA professionals, these stories are a powerful way to learn and understand the basic skills they need in EAP. For experienced practitioners, these stories deepen the understanding of what's possible for clients by revealing layers of complexity in the practice of EAGALA Model work. And for anyone looking to enjoy stories of horses and humans creating relationships, these are stories of hope, humor, and healing.

Make no mistake—the work we do is serious. Our clients come to us in despair and discomfort, in deep pain, and sometimes in tragic circumstances. As we engage the process with our horse facilitators, we also carry the weight of the responsibility to meet these clients with integrity and compassion. But we know that when the EAGALA Model is working at its finest, we create an arena of possibility where people's lives can change. We allow clients to engage the struggle and find the answers for themselves. We know our horses are vital in that process.

No matter who you are—horse lover, curious mental health professional, or full-fledged EAGALA professional—we hope these case stories offer you many insights, along with plenty of surprises and laughter. Within the very serious work we do, there can perhaps be room for the lighthearted and a deeper understanding of the good we create together.

PART I

The Why and What of the EAGALA Model

CHAPTER 1

Why the Horse?

Across a bumpy set of railroad tracks and around a hillside bend outside the small town of Marion, North Carolina, Mark Lytle's third-generation family farm is tucked into the countryside with an assortment of animals that would make Dr. Doolittle proud. Llamas and guinea hens, miniature donkeys, sheep and goats, and even a special-needs Tibetan yak with hip dysplasia roam next to a rambling old country barn. An equally wide assortment of horses is pastured across the road: American Quarter Horses, half Arabians, Arabians from the show ring, Welsh and Dartmoor ponies, miniature horses, and a Haflinger.

Mark Lytle spent many years as an Arabian horse trainer before finding equine-assisted psychotherapy in 2001. He discovered the EAGALA Model while putting together an equine program in a residential treatment facility for sexually abusive and aggressive youth. Over the next few years, he transitioned from training champion show horses to working in residential treatment to building a private EAGALA program of his own: Head, Heart, Hands, and Horses. "In the last fifteen years, my threshold to different things has really broadened," he says. "And I'm really thankful that it has, because I probably missed a lot of what horses can really offer."

Today many animals in the Lytle menagerie are rescues and misfits, especially misfits in the traditional world. A few show horses still live at the farm, working in the show ring part time and working with EAGALA clients the rest. The irony is that many of the program's horses would be considered useless by traditional standards, due to age, injury, abuse, or deformity. However, as many people in the equine-assisted business have learned, these same horses are invaluable in the practice of EAGALA Model work. They don't have to be ridden or shown; they only have to show up in the arena and be what they are: millions of years of evolutionary instinct packaged in a horse's body, always present in the moment, always reading their environment and the body language of creatures around them.

EAGALA horses can be all types. They may be a great riding horse, they may be a show horse, or they may have serious issues, making them unsuitable for anything most people would consider "useful." Often these "unsuitable" horses appear and become the ideal horse for the EAGALA Model. If we give these horses an opportunity, they are able to be productive in other areas.

Zohan is a Saddlebred donated to our program because he was considered a "cull" by the show breeder. In other words, he was either going to come to us or be put down, simply because he had a blemish, a piece of fatty tissue on the bottom of his left eyelid. That one flaw changed the path of his life; anyone's hopes and dreams of making him a world-champion show horse weren't going to happen because of this. Once we had his eye checked out to make sure it wasn't anything serious that would affect his health, we decided to bring him home.

We went to Kentucky to pick him up and found a tall, gangly-looking teenaged horse who didn't quite know how to use his legs. He hadn't been handled much at all. In fact, we had to load him by backing the trailer up to the barn door and just herding him in. We got him home, handled him, and played with him a little bit and found out that this horse had an incredible amount of personality. He is mischievous. He can be pushy, but then he also can be standoffish.

And he has an uncanny way of meeting the clients where they need to be met.

So we arrive at our story, "Don't Mess with Zohan." We had a corporate group come out for an EAGALA team-building session. This particular team was comprised of auditors whose job is to ensure financial and procedural compliance with state rules and regulations. As such, these auditors are rarely welcomed; their job is to go into situations looking for problems. When they find an issue, they need to assert their authority to get it under control. The team was referred to us because of the negative perceptions they encounter in the field and the ways people feel and react to them when they go into an audit. They were seeking to develop more confidence and better understand how they could balance authority with diplomacy to moderate the varying degrees of animosity they encountered.

In the session, Zohan was chosen by a guy who put a halter and lead rope on him and kept a firm hold. We started to notice patterns right away. Throughout this session, Zohan kept taking his mouth and head and putting them on this guy's arm. He couldn't stand still and would jog around him in circles. The client would jerk on Zohan's lead rope and then sometimes just pop him on the neck.

We noticed this and started checking in with him: "How's it going?"

"He's fine. Everything's fine," was the client's response.

Meanwhile, his knuckles were turning white on the lead rope. The horse pushed him. The client pushed back. A tug-of-war got under way, yet when we checked in, everything was "fine." The battle raged: who could be the strongest, who was in control. As Zohan's behavior escalated, the client responded in kind and put his hands on the horse.

Meanwhile the rest of the team all began moving away from the guy and his horse. This guy was saying, "Everything's fine," yet he was holding on with an iron fist, the horse was fighting back, and the team was distancing themselves.

After seeing this for a while, we decided to check in about what was happening between the horse and this client.

After the group discussed the horse's behavior and their response of backing away, the guy shared that he realized he came into the session looking for trouble. He picked Zohan because he thought the horse would be a challenge and that he would have the opportunity to "show" him. He then explained that he came from a law-enforcement background, where he felt compelled to quickly get the upper hand. As a financial auditor, he went into programs in the same way: looking for trouble ahead of time, looking for ways to assert control.

Further discussion revealed a deeper problem: his team admitted that they reacted to him in the field much the same way they reacted in the arena, by distancing themselves from his dominance. Even worse, he tended to meet clients in a way that provoked resistance rather than cooperation. His approach was counterproductive to the team's desire to moderate client reactions and improve the way they handled situations.

The team went on to complete their session and as a result of this encounter were able to pinpoint and articulate a key issue with this particular team member. The team realized this person was perhaps not in an ideal role, and they eventually made changes, moving him into a more appropriate area.

As Zohan so often does, he met the client exactly where he needed to be met, thus bringing an issue to the forefront of the client session. We've seen Zohan interact with clients in a myriad of distinct and diverse ways. And each time, it serves to uncover the issue at hand.

That, to me, is what a good EAGALA horse can do. Pedigree, conformation, and athletic performance don't mean anything here. The horse's presence and natural instincts are all we need.

Distinct and diverse are two key words from this and many stories. In the EAGALA Model of equine-assisted psychotherapy and personal development, the arena becomes a container of sorts, a place where parallels to the client's real-life world can be found. The horses start out loose in the arena, free to engage, ignore, or escape their human counterparts as their interest, instincts, and curiosity dictate. The treatment team sets up the session for the client, but it's the client him- or herself, not the therapy team, who assigns meaning and significance to what evolves for him or her during the session.

The job of the treatment team is to step back and allow the client-horse engagement to develop unimpeded. As the process unfolds, therapist and equine specialist observe the horse's response in the form of both direct and indirect body language, behavior, and interaction with the client. Activity for both horse and client are tracked within a framework of four criteria: Shifts, Patterns, Unique moments and Discrepancies. By paying close attention to these distinctions, the horse's response provides information to the team. These four criteria, or "SPUD'S™," become benchmarks indicating when something of significance is happening.

In the case of Zohan, his responses change in very specific ways from client to client. By trusting the horse and trusting that these responses hold meaning, the team can progress through the session, providing feedback to the client and tracking the client's response in turn.

But again, what the significance of any scenario actually *means* depends entirely on the client. The treatment team will point out SPUD'S and raise questions but refrain from coloring their commentary with personal conclusions. The client's response should always be entirely his or her own.

Why the Horse?

This brings up a key question: What is it about the horses that makes their responses so appropriate? Other animals can certainly be beneficial in therapy situations, so why utilize horses instead of dogs or some other animal? The answer is both simple and complex. Domesticated as the horse may be, it still retains the deeply rooted instincts of a prey animal. For millennia, the horse has survived by being so finely tuned to its environment that the slightest discrepancy in its surroundings evokes immediate response: a bush moves the wrong way; silence is detected where there should be sound. When this happens, the horse bursts into movement, taking immediate and evasive action.

This is very different from dogs, which possess an entirely different set of behaviors—predator behaviors. The horse as prey animal seeks to escape to safety first and ask questions later. When even a small hesitation can mean the difference between life and death, detecting those discrepancies swiftly and reacting within milliseconds becomes key—a survival instinct that remains intact to this day. Being so finely tuned to incongruence makes horses capable of reacting almost instantaneously, sometimes seemingly before an incident occurs in their environment. An entire herd of horses will often react as a cohesive unit, moving as if they possess a single mind and body.

Today horses still respond to incongruence in their environment, no matter what the source, even if it comes from a nearby human. This receptivity and response can be observed by human team members through definitive cues in the equine body language. By knowing their individual horses, team members can recognize Shifts, Patterns, Unique aspects and Discrepancies, which become material for client processing. Many times these reactions are subtle. Other times they are quite overt, as in the case of Twister in a story called "Quarterback Down."

We have several miniature horses, which I use because people's perception of miniature horses is sometimes not the reality. People make all kinds of assumptions because the horse is little, and that creates lots of interesting situations.

We were contacted by the coach of an area high school who wanted to bring his entire football team out to the farm. The kids on the team were in trouble for drinking on the football field. They risked suspension, expulsion, and charges for drinking and vandalism unless they became accountable and owned up to what they had done. All of them were going to be in serious trouble.

So the whole team came out for a session in the arena. The equine herd for that day included a big horse, an average-size horse, a medium-size pony, and a miniature horse named Twister. We started the session by asking them to move the horses around the arena, working as a team to keep them contained.

The team all grabbed hands and formed a circle around the horses. They started having some success moving them around and were able to keep them contained fairly easily. But then we started putting out distractions for the horses: hay, a bucket with apples, some grain, and other stuff. We correlated these to the distractions that got the team into trouble. Keeping the horses away from the food became much more challenging.

Sure enough, the horses started becoming more vocal, nickering and making noises with their mouths. With twenty-one kids in the arena, the circle was pretty big. The big horse and pony walked around the edge of the team, challenging the circle and really trying to break through. The team held fast.

However, Twister had other ideas. He went straight toward the quarterback.

The quarterback was one of the biggest guys out there, and when Twister came toward him, he bent his knees in defensive mode and hollered, "I've got this little thing." Twister ran up to him and wasn't going to be stopped. The way the kid crouched, with his knees bent, allowed Twister to literally go *over* this big kid, knocking him down as if sacking the quarterback, and escape the circle. Exclamations could be heard across the whole arena.

"Wow, what just happened?" we asked.

One kid responded, "That little-bitty horse took out the quarterback! He challenged Johnny the quarterback. *Nobody* challenges Johnny the quarterback." The whole team seemed quite impressed with Twister, sharing the same reaction when they checked in. Everybody, that is, except the quarterback. His face turned red after hearing his teammates' comments, and he walked out of the arena.

It didn't take long for the truth to come out: The quarterback was the one who brought the alcohol to the football field. He was the one who cut the lock on the gate and got the rest of the team in trouble. All of them were being held responsible because they felt like they couldn't confront the quarterback. And yet the littlest horse in the arena had called him out. So after he left the arena, the other twenty kids followed Twister's example and made a plan not to let Johnny the quarterback bully them anymore.

This story is a great illustration of why the EAGALA Model works so well. The human facilitators didn't try to shape outcomes; we simply allowed the horses enough space and time to be themselves, and they did the rest. Because he was allowed his space, Twister *found* a way to take care of himself when he felt compelled to escape the circle. He had the freedom to make it happen. The clients then connected the dots, finding significance in the fact that Twister chose Johnny the quarterback as the weak link in the circle. In their minds, Twister was the one who confronted the bully in their midst and modeled the right behavior for them.

The EAGALA Model is one of the most respectful ways I have ever found to work with horses. Horses have choices; they can check in or check out or be present. Our job is to make sure that, as facilitators, we don't judge those actions. We simply use their actions to frame our questions: "What happened? Where has this happened before? When and how?"

Occasionally we'll have a situation—like the one with Twister or the story that follows—where the horse seems to perform the intervention for us. Their actions may seem positively inspired, when what we're *really* seeing is the horse's ability to recognize and respond to incongruence and nonverbal messages in their environment. Our job, again, is to observe closely enough to recognize the SPUD'S—Shifts, Patterns, and Unique aspects of the horse's nonverbal body language to uncover something happening for the client. The *D* refers to a Discrepancy in the human client's behavior. The SPUD'S are our structure for identifying those occasions when a client is operating in an incongruent state or experiencing a significant moment in the session.

We were working with a family who was part of an intensive in-home program led by a therapist who occasionally brought client families out to the barn for some group and individual treatment. We'd been working with this family for a while. The child was the identified client, but there was always something that didn't seem quite complete about the situation. While we started seeing a lot of changes in the boy, we also began to notice things going on with the parents. There were times we had suspected that Mom was altered in some way, under the influence of drugs or alcohol, but we had been unable to put our fingers on it.

For this particular session, we had a couple of younger horses in the arena along with my Arabian horse, Mon-Jour, who was thirty years old at the time. We asked the boy and his mother to go out and select a horse and then bring the horse to us.

The mom went toward her horse, and the son went to the very far end of the arena. We noticed that the mom seemed to misstep just a little bit as she chose the horse she wanted and started walking toward her son. That's when Mon-Jour seemed to wake up and kick into gear. He wheeled around and pivoted on his hind legs; then he laid his ears back and rushed at the mom and the horse she had. Mom and horse both responded by moving away, and Mon-Jour came to a standstill.

Meanwhile, the son had chosen another horse at the far end of the arena. Mom kept trying to lead her horse down to join him, but the more she tried to move toward her child, the more Mon-Jour tried to head her off. It was like watching a cutting horse: she would move, and he would move, laying his ears back to push her away with his body language every time.

After a while she let go of her horse, who trotted off to join the rest of the horses and her son at the end of the arena. But the pattern continued. Mon-Jour kept her from going anywhere near those other horses and her son, skillfully herding the mom until she had her back up against the fence next to us. Only then did he seem satisfied.

This was a Unique situation, one I had never seen from Mon-Jour before. So we asked the question, "Hey, guys, what's going on with this horse?"

The son, who was about twelve or thirteen, said, "He's keeping her from me."

So we asked, "Why would the horse need to keep her from you?"

The boy didn't bat an eye, responding, "Because she's high."

We turned to the mom. "Hey, Mom, what do you think about that?" At this she admitted to drinking several beers and downing some pills before driving her son over.

For months the intensive in-home team had suspected there was an issue but could never definitively bring it out into the open. No one within the family ever owned it or said anything about it. Upon her confession we made a mandatory report to the Department of Social Services. The dad came to pick up his son, while his mom was taken into custody.

I call this story "Under the Influence" and use it to demonstrate how some situations can truly be unique. Beyond knowing my horse and knowing his behavior that day was unusual, the way he literally *took action* and took matters under his own control to separate a parent under the influence from her child was exceptional. We let the situation play out until it revealed the secret that was hidden.

Over and over again, I've seen horses demonstrate a reaction to incongruence in human clients. When we trust in that reaction and follow the horse's lead, it typically leads to uncovering a Discrepancy, something the client is hiding or was not aware of him- or herself.

Horses are much better at reading situations than we are. Their ability to comprehend discrepancy in their environment—or in this case within a human's body language and nonverbal cues—is extremely accurate. The horse's response gives us information. And yet sometimes *trusting* that response, relying on it as a skeptical human facilitator, can be a challenge. While the examples in these three stories demonstrate some very overt ways the horse can react in client sessions, they also demonstrate how the horses' actions can push the boundaries of our narrow understanding. When we as facilitators trust the horse through this process, what needs to be revealed typically comes forth. From that point, our clients can do the work of making the connections for themselves, of finding their own way. Often it is emotionally safer for clients to talk "through" the horse's behavior, as the last story showed.

The Impact of Herd Behavior

Another key dynamic making horses so suitable for working with humans is their herd behavior. Horse herds have many parallels to human herds. In addition to being essential for survival, the herd serves to fulfill social and emotional needs essential to a balanced existence. Within the herd framework, certain social behaviors are shaped, and a hierarchy of leadership is firmly in place.

In short, horses in a herd act in ways that feel very familiar and relatable to people. People can assign roles to different horses corresponding to their own lives and find meaning to their actions. These parallels often allow the client to see patterns, create metaphors, and find perspective for his or her own situations.

> This is a story I call "Half-Dead Fred." Fred was the very first horse donated to our program to use for EAGALA Model work, and he was in our program for years. Fred was a superstar. He really was great for individual sessions and continually taught us about watching our horses, knowing our horses, and reading our horses.
>
> Fred came to us in his late teens but many years later suffered an injury, a herniated disk in his spine that only allowed him to walk in circles. So we retired Fred and did our best to keep him comfortable.
>
> Eventually, however, he started to deteriorate, losing weight and appearing depressed. As his situation progressed, we gave Fred a horse friend named Gabriel and kept them in a paddock to themselves. We just kind of waited for Fred to tell us when he was ready to go. Eventually his pain became harder to manage, and we knew the time was near.
>
> Fred, however, wasn't quite done.
>
> We had a client, "Tommy," who had been using Gabriel in sessions. This was a client who was identified as a gang member and was engaging in some really risky behavior, including vandalism and graffiti. Mom was concerned and scared for him. In fact, she was participating in our sessions too.
>
> The clients came out for their session one day while Gabriel was hanging out with Fred. Mom, Tommy, and the treatment team decided to go up and get Gabriel out of the pen together. We walked up to the paddock where Fred and Gabriel were. Tommy stepped in to get Gabriel. Fred was doing his usual, walking in circles.

As soon as Tommy moved toward Gabriel, Fred, doing his circle, somehow got in between them. We thought it was purely coincidental and didn't think much of it, but as the boy stepped around Fred to get to Gabriel, Fred did another circle and cut the client off a second time.

This went on for a good half hour. Fred would not let Tommy get close to Gabriel. Every time he approached Gabriel, Fred got in his way. So we checked in with him. "Hey, Tommy, what's going on?"

He said, "Well, Fred won't let me anywhere near my buddy."

We said, "Well, let's talk about your buddy. Who is this that you're trying to get close to?"

He said, "My friends that I hang out with."

We said, "Well, if Gabriel is your friends, your friends in the gang, who or what is Fred that keeps coming in between you?"

Tommy responded, "That's my mom, and my mom always shows up and tries to move me in a different direction away from my friends." He then said, "Mom, will you come in here and help me?"

As soon as Mom entered the arena, Fred stopped moving Gabriel away from Tommy and instead moved Gabriel toward them. Tommy and Mom were able to get Gabriel. Fred kept pushing Mom with his head to move closer to her son.

This story of Fred hits home for me on many levels. This is a horse who wasn't intended to be part of the session. The session wasn't supposed to be in that paddock. We were just going to get Gabriel and move on. Well, Fred took things into his own hands and inserted himself. "Half-Dead Fred" showed up, despite his condition, and did the work. The client then created the metaphor on his own, and a key connection was made between him and his mom.

We have so many reasons and excuses not to show up for sessions. We have some clients who won't come out in adverse conditions—if it's too cold, too hot, or raining. Yet here is this horse, literally on borrowed time, who clocks in and helps move that relationship with mom and son to a totally different level, just really shifts them. In spite of his herniated disk, the walking in circles, and whatever pain he had, Fred didn't let his "stuff" get in the way. It just kind of puts things into perspective for me how powerful *any* horse can be in the moment.

Horses continually test boundaries and negotiate for position within the hierarchy, a behavior that extends to the humans when they enter the horse's environment. The horse often doesn't seem to distinguish between horse and human; if the human is in the horse's vicinity, the horse will often test its boundaries and limits with that human. This is similar to what we do in our own families and social groups. Because of this, horses' natural instincts to assert themselves and test boundaries in their surroundings become a very useful tool for human facilitators.

Some horses push boundaries in ways more overt than others, seeing how far they can go before getting pushback. They respond according to the feedback they receive, which in turn provides information to the human client and the facilitation team. Do the clients recognize when their personal space is being squeezed? How do they respond? Do they overreact or not react at all? How can they moderate their response to change the horse's behavior?

Movement and Response

Horses use movement in the herd to assert themselves; dominant horses will move less-dominant horses around as they wish. Even while playing, the horse that succeeds in making its counterpart move first "wins" the game. The stories about Mon-Jour and Fred above are just two examples. Both horses used their size and body language to move humans around in their environment. In both cases, the horses placed the humans seemingly where they wanted.

Horses evoke response in people, whether that response is curiosity and engagement or fear and intimidation. The horse's large size, specifically, evokes response in multiple ways. This becomes an especially powerful dynamic in the EAGALA Model, where horses are free to move around the arena in a client session. Because the horse is not confined, the client is compelled to pay attention and respond to a horse's movement in the arena, whether it is to move out of the horse's way or move toward the horse to engage.

The dynamic of movement itself is key to the experiential aspect of equine-assisted psychotherapy and is the reason experiential therapy is often so effective: movement impacts our psyche. If the purpose of therapy is to create change, and we look at change as *movement*, a client's physical movement can become a precursor to internal movement or change.

The horse's size and proximity during a session get us to move our bodies. We as human facilitators can use the idea of movement during the client session to assess when and where shifts might be happening with the client. Likewise, we can assess the movement of the horses during the session to detect shifts as well—Shifts that might not be visibly apparent in the human client become apparent through the horse.

The horse's size can create other parallels in a therapy context. To some clients, the horse's large size can represent fears or obstacles that seem too large to overcome. The task then becomes that of helping the client develop skills to move those embodied fears through moving the horse around in the arena. In the experiential setting of the EAGALA Model, clients can experiment until they actually find the right balance of action and assertiveness to successfully move the horse through the arena.

Relationship and Connection

Dogs tend to want to be near humans; they seem to seek human companionship. Horses, on the other hand, seem much more ambivalent and independent of humans. They don't necessarily seek approval or companionship in the way dogs seem to do. If you want to create a relationship with a horse, you need to provide a compelling reason to connect. For that reason, when a horse *does* choose to connect with us, the moment seems remarkable and powerful.

Those who work around horses know how amazing this form of connection can feel. Once they achieve it successfully, they strive to create that connection again and again. It can be equally powerful for clients, many of whom know only disconnection, dysfunction, or toxicity in their lives, when they have relationships at all.

Horses create opportunity for relationships, but a relationship with a prey animal can be challenging. The horse's agenda first includes finding safety, food, and comfort in its environment. When these needs are met, horses become responsive to other dynamics. They become curious. They experiment with boundaries. They negotiate hierarchy and respond to leadership.

The human must explore ways to create that connection and align him- or herself to the horse's particular psychology and language. If the human client is successful setting up an interaction to achieve response and connection without producing threat, fear, or discomfort for the horse, those skills can transfer to creating connection in the human world.

Human interactions are filled with bias and judgment; we use them constantly to filter our interactions and qualify relationships. Horses lack these biases and judgments. For many people who struggle with relationship skills, this makes horses emotionally safer to engage. Human clients working to build those skills in EAGALA sessions learn that the horse will show them when they've reached the right balance of assertiveness and collaboration. What am I doing when I cause the horse to move away from me? What elicits a positive response? How do I achieve connection?

As we explore the EAGALA Model through these stories in the coming chapters, observe how the many dynamics of the horse come together to make the client-horse connection extremely powerful in a therapy setting. Note the many times verbal communication is outweighed by nonverbal communication in the session experience. Over and over again, you will see how layers within the process unfold while they continually test the growth and learning of its human facilitators as well.

CHAPTER 2

The Arena and Its Parallel to Life

In life, growth and learning happen throughout our journey, shaped by the container of our individual experience. Each of us has to solve our own challenges and find solutions within a continuum of success, failure, struggle, and resolution.

The same principle applies in the EAGALA Model. At all times, we trust that the client holds within his or her struggle the needed solutions. Like life itself, this process is often messy and imperfect. Our goal is not to make things easier or to create short-term fixes but to facilitate a scenario wherein the client can move toward long-term solutions and skills. Facilitators must create a setting wherein the client can move, practice, and learn resilience and problem-solving skills while working through these struggles.

This active, immersive process is called an "experiential" modality. Through the various dynamics made possible by the horse, the EAGALA Model sets the stage to evoke metaphor, response, and movement in the client. The facilitating team then initiates the therapeutic process with questioning and reflective listening to spark insight and discovery. The experiential process involves active experimentation as the client harnesses new understanding and adjusts his or her behavior and response to the horse.

Above all, the experiential model is physical. It's all about doing versus talking, giving each client the opportunity to explore and learn. Facilitators focus on setting up activities that reveal and *show*. The EAGALA Model process is about keeping focus on what actually happens in the session, versus engaging in what *doesn't* happen, what *might* happen, or what *should* happen.

I call this story "The *Groundhog Day* Kid," and it illustrates what can happen when we make the mistake of judging success or failure by focusing on the activities in session instead of the process. This story shows how easy it is to let other things influence the client's story.

We had a client from the Department of Juvenile Justice who was starting work to transition back into the community. He was supposed to come out and work with horses on activities that could parallel the issues he might encounter in the real world. This experience would be the first time since being locked up that he was brought off campus, which is why he got out of the van in an orange jumpsuit, shackled with cuffs on his hands, his feet, and around his waist. The chains were all connected as he shuffled through the gate and out into the pasture, where they removed the chains so our first exercise could take place.

For our first activity, we gave him instructions to catch and halter one of the horses and bring the horse back to us. He took the halter and lead rope from my hand and walked out. He then proceeded to just kind of meander around the horses for a whole hour without approaching one. After an hour, he came back, and we asked him, "What happened out there?" and he said, "Nothing."

We invited him to elaborate on "nothing," but he did not say anything more. He left the pasture, they put the cuffs back on him, and back he went to detention. Next week he came out again, and the process repeated itself: he went out and wandered around the horses for an hour without being very verbal or really approaching a horse.

Twelve *weeks* later, the licensed mental health professional and I were growing impatient and worried that anything was going to progress with this client—at least in the way we were defining "progress." He was still doing the same thing over and over and over, just like the movie *Groundhog Day*.

By the thirteenth week, we were struggling whether to have the client continue to come. Aside from being frustrating, this happened to also be our first client from the Department of Justice. We wanted the process to have good results. We wondered what this referral source was thinking and if they thought this might be a waste of time, since it seemed like the same thing was happening week to week.

However, through it all his clinical supervisor kept bringing him back, saying, "You guys don't understand. This young man has never maintained a level status this long. To be allowed to leave campus for thirteen weeks, he's had to maintain the highest level of good behavior status, and he has never done that before. I don't care what the heck you're doing out there. Keep it up."

That week, it took the client a little longer to get out of the van. Impatient, I dropped the lead rope and halter by my feet. He came up to us, and I said, "Just go out there and bring a horse back." He picked up the halter and lead rope, looked at us, and walked through the gate. But he only walked in a few feet before opening up his hand and letting the halter and lead rope go. He then proceeded to walk out into the pasture and right up to the hardest horse to catch, a horse named Red. Red was the kind of horse who always moved away and didn't seem to show much interest in engaging with humans. The client put his hand out, and Red put his chin right into the man's palm and followed him all the way up to the gate and into the barnyard, where we were standing.

Considering this horse, this was Unique and impressive. "Wow. What was different today?" we asked, and he replied, "You didn't tell me that I had to shackle them today. I won't do that to anybody."

Thirteen weeks—this client had been riding back and forth from the farm for thirteen weeks inside that van, with shackles coming and going. "Catch and halter a horse" seemed pretty simple and straightforward, but for him it wasn't straightforward at all. The halter and lead rope were shackles to him. He didn't appear to be doing anything out there, but he was doing everything possible back at the jail to be able to come back. He was making darn sure that he came back so nobody else could shackle those horses.

This was a client who had never done anything consistent before. It was powerful learning for us and him. How much sooner could we have helped him move forward if we hadn't been handing him the very tools creating the roadblock to progress?

Undoubtedly, despite the roadblock we created, things were happening in the sessions. While he may not have been "catching and haltering" a horse, there were relationships building and skills developing that impacted his ability to work with Red the way he did. There were things happening to cause the changes in his behavior at the detention center. Because of this experience, we learned how the way we set up our sessions can really impact clients.

This story illustrates how the shape of the "container" we choose and how we use it impacts the client dynamic. In the "*Groundhog Day* Kid" story, we were telling the client to evolve his story using the rope and halter as simple tools—without recognizing at the time that the rope and halter themselves were part of his story. Was he being the *Groundhog Day* kid, or were we being the *Groundhog Day* facilitators?

Every aspect of the EAGALA Model "physicalizes" the client's conscious and unconscious experiences. The horses, the props, and the session tasks provide the storyboard, waiting in readiness for the client's story to unfold and to take on meaning for the client. The arena becomes a microcosm of the client's life, the container where parallels to the client's real-life world can be found. In order for the session to be about the client's story, as facilitators we want to be especially cautious of directing clients toward any potential symbols or "characters" on that storyboard. In the case of the *Groundhog Day* Kid, the facilitators learned a key lesson when they directed the client to use a halter and lead rope.

Allowing the Inside World Out

Metaphor is a foundation of the EAGALA Model. In the arena, client-identified metaphors help unlock the unconscious so clients can define, verbalize, and understand the internal issues and dynamics they're unaware of. Metaphor helps clients transform abstract concepts and feelings into physical and concrete characteristics that can be observed, moved, touched, and changed. For example, it is one thing for a person to talk about his or her sadness and another for sadness to be represented through a horse or other symbol in the environment that the client can now address in a tangible and outside-perspective way.

Everything in the client session has potential to be a metaphor: the horses, the props, and the space. The treatment team draws out the symbolism through a questioning model designed to help the client make physical the abstract. We do this by drawing attention to the physical aspects we note in both the client and in the horses through the SPUD'S framework mentioned earlier. We create dialogue around the aspects of SPUD'S and allow clients to define the meaning around them.

In most sessions, the goal is to allow this to happen in a natural, non-directive manner, which the treatment team works to recognize and use. In other scenarios, the facilitators set up the metaphor deliberately to match treatment goals. If the client indeed follows that direction during the session, specific and defined aspects can be the focus.

However, the key word here is *if*. The facilitating team needs to be ready and willing at all times to abandon the intended metaphor when the client takes things in a different direction. In a solution-oriented model like EAGALA, our understanding of the intended plan may not be what manifests for the client. At all times the client is the one who assigns meaning and identifies the parallels. Session activities always have the potential to lead clients to experience a part of their lives, their reality, in ways we can't anticipate.

> This is a story I call "Marching to the Beat of a Different Drummer," about an adolescent client I'll call "Alex." In junior high, Alex got into trouble and was labeled "the Bathroom Bandit" because he loved to vandalize the school bathrooms.
>
> When he was fourteen, his mom took him and his sister Christmas shopping in the mall. He went into the restroom and was gone a very long time. Mom was getting ready to go in after him when he came out. "What were you doing in the bathroom?"

she asked, assuming that he had once again been vandalizing a public bathroom.

But he said, "I was just raped."

His mom said, "You're lying. If I have to pay to have this bathroom redone, you're going to be in trouble. I am going to press charges."

The boy insisted, "No, I've been raped."

On the way home, he got more and more upset, but his mom refused to believe him. A few days later, he came to his mom and showed her that he was bleeding from his rectum. At this point they took him to the hospital where, sure enough, they found multiple bruises and other signs to confirm that he had indeed been raped.

Far from starting the road to recovery, he instead stopped talking over the course of the next few days; he quit communicating verbally entirely. With an IQ of 143 and no history of autism, he was diagnosed with trauma-based selective mutism.

Alex was sixteen by the time he was referred to us. He had been to three different therapists in three different therapy models and was nonresponsive to all of them. At the time of his first session, I was curious about how the therapy process was going to work with someone who would not talk to us at all. But then I thought, *Well, horses are 100 percent nonverbal, so maybe this will work.*

Alex arrived for his first session. He came in but would not give us eye contact. We did notice, however, that he had a cell phone. Normally we didn't allow electronic devices in the session. While it annoyed me that he was bringing this in with him, the mental health therapist suspected that, with this client's issues about talking, the phone might be an important part of the story.

We asked him to go out and introduce himself to the horses. Throughout the whole session, the client did everything we asked him to do. Yet every time we checked in and gave him the opportunity to talk about his experience, he would click on his smartphone and blast music at us at top volume. The sound bounced off the rounded walls of my arena. I found myself getting aggravated, and I was interpreting this as a disrespectful way to say he was not going to talk to us. This was a client who had a history of being a trouble-maker and not respecting property. That knowledge fueled my irritation even further and reinforced my belief that he was playing games with us.

This continued; we would ask him a question, and he would play a song. I was feeling, *This isn't working. He just seems to be getting worse.* By the third session, he was playing this loud music throughout most of the session. Yet, despite that, the horses were following him with the music, doing all kinds of cool stuff. He did everything we asked him to do—everything but talk.

Then along about the sixth session, something happened. I asked, "How was it today?" I don't know why the question was any different than any other day, but for once I was really listening. He turned toward me and played "Pretty Good for the Shape I'm In," by Joe Nichols. It was like a tractor trailer just ran over me. I realized Alex was communicating with me. Right behind that, both the therapist and I realized, *Wow! He's been talking to us the whole time!*

Just to be sure, we asked him a couple more questions, and each time he responded with a song. It was just amazing. What was interesting was that the horses were very intrigued by the smartphone and were responding. We started to watch him very carefully, and you know, he had a song for everything. He had different songs for different horses. When he approached them, he played their songs. Later on we noticed that he had different songs for each emotion he was feeling.

He had been communicating with us every single time we asked. When he realized that we were finally understanding his communication patterns, he played a song named "It's About Time" or something along those lines. He immediately relaxed with us.

All along that loud music should have disturbed the horses, but here's where it got interesting. The horses were completely compliant, no matter what we asked him to do. I deliberately put horses into his sessions who wouldn't respond in the presence of any incongruence. But when he walked into that arena, those horses greeted him and circled him. He was part of the herd like no other client has ever been. The only difference was that he wasn't talking or verbalizing to us. Not talking was congruent for him. It just didn't look like we really wanted it to look.

So we started asking him what sounds the horses liked that day, and he would play some song back. He was telling his story very clearly, and wherever he went those horses went. When I showed interest in his music selection, he showed me twenty-five hundred songs on his smartphone. He had used them so much, he knew which songs went where to communicate what he wanted without having to talk. I thought it was an ingenuous coping mechanism.

This case really impacted us as facilitators. This was a great lesson for me and my MH partner about assumptions and labels. We both realized our mistake at about the same time. The amazing part is that if we had truly been looking at the horses more carefully, listening, and being present, we would probably have figured it out in the first session. We were so caught up in our stuff, we weren't truly taking the cue from the horses, who weren't upset at all by the loud music. They were pointed in the right direction the whole time. That is my only regret. Sometimes we are really wrong in our assumptions.

As for Alex, he did eventually talk again. It started with non-verbal gestures and shrugs, then progressed to verbal communication to the horses. Over a period of sessions, he expanded to talking to us and, eventually, to others in his life.

This case story is a vibrant example of how communication doesn't have to come in the form of talking. Sometimes client metaphor is expressed in unusual or distinct ways, even ways that don't use words. Listening sometimes comes in the form of allowing whatever is being brought into the arena to play out and reveal the symbolism it holds.

Understanding the importance of how everything in the arena space can potentially be a symbol in the client's metaphor is the key for this story. The smartphone was an important character that had a primary and meaningful role. The horses didn't put judgments on that role like the facilitators were doing. So often we place our own meanings on the symbols instead of truly listening to what the meaning is for the clients.

"Marching to the Beat of a Different Drummer" is also a case in which the client's tool for creating metaphor was brought into the session from the outside world—via his smartphone.

When creating the space for client sessions, deciding what is going to be allowed or put into that space needs to be carefully thought out. Entering the symbolic world means that typical horsemanship tools are not needed or necessary. The possible number of resources that can be used in the space as potential symbols is almost limitless. Possible objects include cones, poles, swim noodles, and Hula-Hoops. These items provide a range of colors, shapes, and sizes and can hold any kind of meaning.

Additionally, more potentially direct symbols may be put in the space, symbols that have relevance to the client: boots and helmets for military clients; dolls and stuffed animals for family work; chairs, paper, and office supplies for corporate work.

It makes sense that objects brought in by the clients can become a part of the space, as their stories and the role those objects play are already under way before they even step into the space.

When it comes to personal devices and other objects, there's no doubt practitioners are seeing the effect of electronics and digital media specifically; these items are adding a whole new dynamic to our relationships and interactions with the world, including creating another class of addictive behaviors. Allowing cell phones or other electronics to be brought in by the clients is part of the parallel to life. It is interesting to see what part those electronic characters play in the unfolding story and in the relationships with the horses. Some EAGALA practitioners keep a bucket of old phones and electronic objects on hand as potential resources because of the primary role these devices have in our lives today.

This story is called "Texting Mom." We got a call from a mom wanting to bring her family out and work on being more connected. Her kids were growing into teenagers, and she felt like the family was drifting apart and not really communicating. She said she was really frustrated that the kids were consumed with their cell phones and not engaging as a family.

For the first session, with the identified goal focused on "connecting," we just asked them to go introduce themselves to the horses and see if they connected with one horse more than the others. Right away it was interesting that the three high-school-aged kids all stayed together and that the horses kind of circled them. The mom stayed separate and wasn't even near a horse. When we checked in, the kids shared that they were doing their thing, and Mom was over there doing her thing, and the horses thought that they (the kids) were more interesting. Mom shared that this was the typical scenario at home: the kids were always off doing their thing while she was on the outside.

In the second session, we checked in about thoughts on the previous session. The kids said, "We didn't intentionally leave Mom out. We think Mom sets herself out a lot." Mom was surprised and didn't agree with that. Mom had brought the kids in because she thought *they* were the ones disconnecting. She didn't want to get called out herself.

We then had them do a task in which they had to create a place where they all could come together—horses, kids, and mom—without touching the horses in any way and without talking. We chose these rules because we noticed that everybody talked at one time, constantly interrupting and trying to answer for each other. Previously, the kids had been touching the horses quite a lot. So we thought we would explore what "coming together" would look like when removing these commonly used and sometimes abused tools of "connection"—namely, touch and talking.

The family went out, and the kids started moving toward the horses. The horses started moving away from them and then stopped. The kids then built a circle out of PVC pipe and tried to move the horses into the circle. The horses started moving faster. Mom tried to step in front of them, using her hands to signal "slow down." The kids kept on going, trying to herd the horses into the circle.

This went on for about forty minutes. It wasn't totally chaotic, but the horses ended up running and moving around the space with the kids running after them. Then we noticed that Mom had turned her back toward us. She was using her cell phone! All of a sudden, the kids stopped and started pulling out their phones and looking at them.

From that point forward, things really changed. The kids slowed down and came over to stand with their mom inside the circle. Then all of the horses came to them and stood inside the circle too. The kids looked at their phones again as Mom typed. They all left the circle, and the horses followed them. Then they came back to the circle, and the horses followed them back in, putting their noses toward the people.

The whole thing was really interesting. We checked in. "What happened out there?"

Mom burst into tears. "We're a family, and we do come together when it matters." When we asked her to tell us more, Mom said she had been resentful and blaming the kids—and their cell phones—for the distance.

Mom said that standing inside the circle and seeing the horses moving around and around showed her two things. One was that she felt like their lives were spent running in circles. The second was that when she was inside the circle, with the kids on the outside, she suddenly knew what to do to get their attention. She reached for the tool she knew would work: her cell phone. Suddenly it all came together.

When she finally used her own cell phone to text them, she realized they actually did listen and that she could get them to work together. The realization was that they *were* connected as a family and that their cell phones were actually helping them stay connected. Even more than that, Mom relied on their cell phones to know where all of her kids were and what they were doing at any given time. The connection just wasn't in a form she expected. Now she could harness it even further, using the phones to take charge and tell the kids when to come home for dinner or meet somewhere.

This realization wasn't a huge thing; it was a shift, allowing her to reframe everything. When she stepped outside of things, she realized she needed to embrace her family's technology and use it in a positive way.

This family came two more times. By the third session they were completely different. Mom was in the middle of the kids, and she stayed in the center of their circle. When we checked in, Mom verified, "We're together. It may not look like I want it to look sometimes, but we are a strong family." They didn't have to stay in therapy for long; four sessions were all it took to let them figure it out on their own.

Tying It Together

No matter what happens in the arena—good, bad, or unexpected—a good facilitating team will find a way to use it. Such developments become part of the story when they happen, even though those distractions are often not what we expect, want, or plan. Part of creating space for clients and allowing them to figure things out on their own means accommodating a myriad of unplanned possibilities that might interject themselves into the session. In nearly every case, clients are able to tie the arena experience back into their life experience.

Experiential models provide clients the opportunity to experience their life. Through the EAGALA Model, the arena creates a space to "physicalize" the client's internal world, moving the abstract and the internal into the concrete. Allowing clients to project their experience onto outer symbols enables them to put things outside themselves, where they can work on them, confront them, shift and release them. This is called self-distancing, which we'll discuss again in more detail.

Metaphors work because they transform a client from simply relating to horses to a client connecting with deeper meaning in life.[2] Once the client begins assigning roles and meaning to the elements within the sessions, our traditional labels for the horses and their equipment no longer matter. Once the metaphors arise, what matters is the meaning assigned by the client. In between moments of observation, processing, clarification, and reflection, the facilitators continually invite the client back into the experience with the horses and into their storyboard. In this way, change occurs naturally as the client becomes more conscious of the storyline evolving in his or her symbolic world.[3]

However, as you'll see in the coming chapters, the challenge for the treatment team is to always make the clients' experience about *their* story, with their meaning. The team is not there to change the client's metaphor or in any way place the team's agenda on it. "Your purpose is not to analyze or interpret the clients' experience. It is not even to understand it. Rather, it is to offer them the opportunity to become aware of their symbolic perceptions with minimal 'contamination' by your metaphors."[4]

---

2 EAGALA, *Fundamentals of the EAGALA Model*, 92.

3 Ibid., 95.

4 James Lawley and Penny Tompkins, *Metaphors in Mind: Transformation Through Symbolic Modelling* (London: The Developing Company Press, 2000), 27.

PART II

The Tools

Four Key Standards of the EAGALA Model

1. Team Approach
All EAGALA sessions involve a team of credentialed, licensed mental health professionals, qualified equine-specialist professionals, horses, and the client(s).

2. Ground Based
No horseback riding is involved. Instead, ground-based experiences are utilized, where the horses become metaphoric of other relationships and areas of life.

3. Code of Ethics
EAGALA has high standards of practice and ethics and an ethics committee and protocol for upholding these standards, ensuring best practices and the highest level of care.

4. Solution Oriented
The basis of the EAGALA Model is a belief that all clients have the best solutions for themselves when given the opportunity to discover them. Therapy-focused experiences allow clients to explore, problem solve, overcome challenges, and discover.

The EAGALA Model SPUD'S
Framework for Observation

S = Shifts
P = Patterns
U = Unique
D = Discrepancies
'S = Self-awareness, or "my stuff"

CHAPTER 3

A Closer Look at the EAGALA Model

The EAGALA Model truly is unique in the mental health world. It is also truly distinct among the modalities of equine-assisted practice. Its clear set of professional standards ensures the emotional health of the human client, but its experiential framework also permits tremendous flexibility in execution, nuance, and interpretation. It allows the human client remarkable latitude to discover, learn, and grow from the horse-human relationship.

Early forms of equine-assisted practice consisted of therapeutic riding and hippotherapy (physical therapy using horses). Those working in these modalities began to recognize generalized improvements in mood and behavior when human clients interacted with horses, often noticing how horses helped people with mental and behavioral health issues. It was logical to begin focusing more and more on the mental health value of equine-assisted work. Various forms of practice evolved, moving from observation of improvement to specific methods of harnessing its potential for mental health benefits.

EAGALA started as a basic experiential model in a ranch setting, one that combined a wilderness component with horses. Its founders were among those who began expanding into other areas of human development. They quickly discovered that working with horses in a mental health context was extremely powerful. Client issues could arise easily and with an intensity, depth, and impact not typically experienced in traditional therapy.

But with this observation came the realization of immense responsibility. When the client issues rose to the surface in a session, the need arose to handle the client's emotional safety with appropriate skill, necessitating the presence of a mental health professional. The utilization of horses necessitated the presence of an equine specialist.

With this realization, EAGALA's two-person, on-the-ground core tenets were born.

Around this time, equine-assisted psychotherapy (EAP) as a concrete model emerged into the mental health world and, not surprisingly, was regarded as a novel technique at best. Those experiencing the work quickly saw its potential. But if EAP was to evolve as a valid and respected treatment model, there had to be clear structure that created the highest level of professionalism and proficiency, to remove all doubt. The need for guidelines, oversight, and quality control; legal and ethical standards; and qualified, professionally trained facilitators was evident.

EAGALA was formally founded in 1999 as a nonprofit 501(c)3 organization. With its creation, it began meeting the need for resources, education, and professionalism in the fields of EAP and EAL. Today, EAGALA has grown to more than forty-five hundred members in fifty countries. The EAGALA Model is garnering respect among those in the mental health world who are discovering the benefits of equine-assisted practice. Its roots and principles are firmly grounded in psychotherapy, and its structure maintains a high level of feedback-driven professionalism as a core principle.

The Four Keys of EAGALA Model Practice

Key One: Team of Two

For a multitude of reasons, the EAGALA Model incorporates a team structure that always includes an equine specialist (ES) and a mental health professional (MH). Whether working in an EAP or EAL context, the inherent power of the equine-based modality creates situations that can become quite personal and intense for the human client. Because of the manner in which horses tap the unconscious, it is not uncommon to have significant emotional reactions or issues arise during a session, necessitating the training and background of a mental health professional. Likewise, EAGALA has standards for the ES. In addition to EAGALA training, this includes education and demonstrated competence working with horses and an understanding of their subtle behaviors and personalities.

First and foremost, the EAGALA Model's two-person format is set up to identify and address these moments in a way that takes into account the emotional needs of the client and approaches them within the legal and ethical laws and boundaries specific to those emotional issues. It is the MH's scope to know what to do and to be legally accountable for handling it properly. This is why having an MH present at all times is an important EAGALA standard for the professionalism, quality, and accountability of services being provided.

Secondly, EAGALA sessions are multifaceted. The horse-client relationship yields a depth and volume of information from both the horse and human client in a multitude of moment-by-moment dynamics. The quality of any given session depends on the facilitating team capturing and responding to the vast amounts of material and the multitude of nonverbal cues playing out. In essence, there is too much for one person to see, and two sets of eyes can accomplish this to a much higher standard.[5] Two sets of eyes mean fewer things get missed; there are two people to capture and coordinate the flow of information, one coming from the horses and one coming from the humans.

Last, and perhaps most valuable, is the ability of the two-person team to minimize some of the common dynamics that can take place in traditional therapy, including client-facilitator imbalances of power;

---

5 EAGALA, *Fundamentals of the EAGALA Model,* 20.

countertransference; or the ability of a facilitator's beliefs, perceptions, or inherent inclinations to impact the client. All of these dynamics have the potential to affect the session and shut down the flow of information being presented.

To be truly effective in this therapeutic environment, facilitators must learn to always work together and be truly present, fluid, and observant. For equine professionals and mental health professionals alike, working as co-facilitators can prove challenging; it's outside the box of traditional training models in both fields. Both parties often need to shift their paradigms completely.

Facilitators need to learn how to handle situations as a team, including a treatment-savvy client's ability to manipulate the dynamics during the session or exploit the facilitators. While working with clients, the facilitator's personal bias and countertransference issues can easily arise, as they do in the following story.

> When you're working in this field, you need to balance between having your emotions impact the session versus staying congruent and real. When I first started doing this work, I'd really empathize when things started getting very tough for a client. My own story would show up as classic countertransference. I call this story "The Girl Who Cried Wolf."
>
> In the beginning, I'd worked in a residential setting with adolescent males, so that's where my comfort level was. But when we started doing outpatient work, lo and behold, the first client brought a group of six adolescent girls out to the farm. Nonetheless, I felt confident. I was the father of my own daughter, after all.

In our first session, the girls came out, we checked in, and got to work. Things went along, and I recall that at one point my miniature horse, Twister, got close to one girl, who started crying. But we went through with the session, and afterward I was feeling pretty good; I thought it had gone well.

But my MH partner thought otherwise. "Mark, what was going on with you?"

I said, "What do you mean?"

She said, "Well, when that girl started crying, you moved away from me and actually stood in between her and Twister. What was up with that?"

I countered, "You are out of your mind. That did not happen." In my mind, I wasn't aware of any such thing or of moving closer.

So we kind of argued, and she said, "You moved," and I was in total denial: "No, I didn't."

The second session, the girl came in with the group again. She barely got through the gate before she started wailing. Of course, Twister, the miniature nuisance, went beelining toward her and rubbed up against her, causing even more tears.

All of a sudden, I felt this immense pain running down my arm. I turned around to find my partner holding the skin on my arm and twisting the heck out of it. I then further realized I was standing *right beside* the crying girl, with my arm about to go around her shoulders. As the MH twisted my arm even further, I took in the whole picture. I had indeed moved away from my partner again.

At this point, I moved from pre-awareness into awareness. I saw exactly what I was doing, although I still didn't know why I was doing it. Through the pain I owned, "Yes, I moved closer to the client." I was going to hug this young lady.

With that, my partner said, "Well, Mark, think about what's going on for you."

I went home that day to find my mom and two adult nieces in a pretty heated conversation, with some yelling going on. I immediately jumped in. "OK, everybody, to your corners! What's going on?" I jumped right in, divided, and conquered until I got things straightened out.

That night, at three o'clock in the morning, it hit me. I sat straight up in bed in a flash of insight and then picked up the phone and called my therapist partner. "I got it! I know what it is!" I said.

She said, "Great, now what are you going to do with it?" and hung up the phone.

I live on the farm with my extended family, which at that time included my dad, my mom, my sister, two adult nieces, my wife, my two daughters, and my mother-in-law. What I realized is that when females are upset in my family, I move closer to fix it. If I don't fix it, I have to go hide because things can get chaotic and out of control.

So the next time we met, I understood this dynamic more, and we sorted it out. My therapist partner asked, "Mark, how do you know the difference when your daughter needs you to move in and make everything OK, and when you need to back off and let her cry it out and figure things out on her own?"

I said, "That's easy—when she's trying to get her way after I'm settled on something."

She said, "The next time in session, really look and watch and think about the difference between when your daughter needs you to move in and take care of her and when she doesn't. I'm going to follow your lead on this. If you want to move closer, we're going to move closer together. If you want to move back, we'll move back."

As we started up for the session, she said, "Don't forget to look at the big picture." As the girls entered the arena, my partner pulled out a double-ended metal snap. She snapped one end to her belt loop and the other to mine so we were hooked together.

Sure enough, the girls barely got through the gate, and water-works started as soon as Twister made a beeline for that same little girl. All of a sudden, I felt a tug; I was already moving forward! And instantly I moved from pre-awareness to awareness to understanding; I was feeling that internal urge to move forward. As soon as I felt that tug, I moved back. And when I moved back, I happened to look at the big picture: I had five other horses in the arena, two of which I know are very tuned in to client emotions, especially when the clients are struggling or expressing authentic emotion. Both of these horses had their butts turned toward this girl and were as far away from her as they could get. While she was crying and wailing away, her peers and all of the horses were far away.

I looked at the situation and whispered to my partner, "Let's back off a little bit." As soon as we backed up, the girl looked up, stopped the waterworks, and then put her head down and wailed even louder. So then we moved even farther away, to the very end of the arena. The girl repeated the pattern about four times and then finally moved a little closer, put her hands on her hips, and said, "What the heck's wrong with you today?"

I only said, "You're good. You've got me."

At that point, she winked at me and never once cried in session again.

This client's *modus operandi* was playing the role of "pitiful me" in many situations. Her mom had passed away two years earlier. At home, she stepped right up and was very involved, helping her younger siblings. But school was a different story. She had her teachers convinced she wasn't handling her grief well. They started letting her take all of her lunches in the teachers' lounge. Eventually it got to the point where she was in the lounge most of the day. They brought her food from takeout and let her watch soap operas. They were completely snowed. She was now in our group because her father had heard these stories from her teachers and wanted to get to the bottom of things.

Over time, the girl realized she didn't want to keep the lie going and asked us how she could redo everything at school so that she was acting more like the way she was at home. So we started seeing her in individual outpatient sessions, and eventually she brought two of those teachers in. We asked her how she wanted to explain what was going on, and she separated the arena into "home" and "school." Then she did charades with the horses, acting out how she was at home versus how she was at school and what she got out of it.

At the end of the session, there were two upset teachers, as they realized what had happened. It turns out her mother had been really involved in the school, volunteering and coaching. So the teachers knew the mom and were her friends. When she first passed away, the girl's homeroom teacher and guidance counselor noticed how hard it was for her to sit in the lunchroom with people coming up to share condolences, so they invited her to the teachers' lounge. Over a two-year period, they compensated for their own grieving by allowing her to manipulate them more and more. It was not that the daughter had not moved through the grief; it was the teachers who had not found closure.

This is just one illustration of how my own lack of self-awareness could have kept this girl stuck in a pattern. Had we not been working in a two-person team, I would not have recognized what was going on. When I caught it, we were able to unravel the whole story. It was a pivotal learning experience for me. I was into fixing problems for people, and this young lady brought it to the forefront. Nowadays, before I move closer to a client, I observe myself first and ask, *What's happening to me? Are my ears getting red? Is my stomach turning?* I work to be more aware.

In short, the two-person model is both professional and practical, creating a safer physical and emotional backdrop for clients, an enhanced ability to respond in situations (including crisis situations), and ongoing feedback and balance to the facilitators.

The safety and effectiveness of the EAGALA Model—and the two-person process—enhance its credibility as an emerging field of therapeutic practice. EAP is still easily misunderstood in the professional therapy world. Adhering to and exhibiting a high level of professionalism remain critical to EAGALA's acceptance and growing validity. This is why EAGALA standards do not compromise or dilute the model simply to accommodate financial limits, outside pressures, and/or limited resources.[6]

Facilitator Training

EAGALA's standards outline professional requirements for both members of the facilitating team. The mental health professional needs to be licensed and credentialed in his or her state or country. The equine specialist is required to have extensive hands-on and educational hours in the equine field.

The EAGALA Model trains its facilitators using the experiential model itself. Reaching a level of proficiency is not a one-time, direct-line process; it involves returning to Part I, II, and Advanced Trainings multiple times to gain insight, experience, and understanding. Practitioners learn more every time they attend the EAGALA trainings.

For a credentialed and highly trained mental health professional, many ingrained principles go right out the window. The horse is the focus of the client relationship, not the therapist. It means giving away a certain amount of control and power to a thousand-pound, nonverbal being.

While the schools of training are more formal for a mental health professional, the levels of indoctrination and structure can be just as hard to loosen. The dynamics of traditional therapy models at times vary greatly from dynamics in an experiential, solution-oriented model. The setting, the approach, and the client-therapist relationship all differ from what traditional therapists are taught. In fact, the client-therapist relationship is totally minimized, and power is given to the horse-client relationship instead.

---

6 EAGALA, *Fundamentals of the EAGALA Model*, 20.

Some therapists struggle to develop trust that everything that needs to happen can truly come through the horses. Most therapists initially struggle even to understand what horse behaviors mean and to acknowledge that those behaviors can *have* meaning. Therapists who've never spent significant time around horses have many preconceived notions about the animals and how they're supposed to act. Safety, and how safety is learned by the client, is another area of concern that typically needs to be shifted significantly.

EAGALA trainers have identified these and several other typical areas of "untraining" for mental health professionals, which often include:

- Remembering that in an office, everything is about developing rapport between therapist and client; in the arena, it is about rapport between client and horse.
- Learning to work in a team with an ES and horses. Most traditional therapists are used to working alone in client settings.
- Going into "talk therapy" mode by processing through in-office methods instead of experiential processing that uses the horse as the focus. What is being projected through the horses and space is the focus.
- Giving control to the horse; trusting that horses alone can influence insight and change in the client. This includes a shift from "direct-line" thinking to "indirect" thinking, trusting that something is happening even during periods of perceived inactivity.
- Letting go of the agenda—and the need to "do more"—during the session; letting go of what we think the client is supposed to learn and the timeframe to learn it in, and instead validating where the client is versus pushing toward a solution.
- Allowing the horse to help the client see the way versus doing the work of helping the client see the way. This requires removing the urge to step in and "help," prompt, or assist in providing solutions to the client. The team has to hold the space for clients to have safe exploration in finding their solution, not lead them. *Process* is where the clients learn, not from the skills "taught."

The following input comes from the perspective of an EAGALA MH professional, trainer Brenda Hunter:

In my first encounter, I saw one of my long-term clients make more progress after fifteen minutes in the arena than she'd made the past year in my office. I couldn't believe how quickly the intervention worked. I was so wowed by my first encounter, I became gung ho to learn everything I could about the EAGALA Model and was very excited and eager to put it into practice.

The biggest challenge in my own untraining was letting go of interpreting so much of what people would tell me. Even when I learned to physically step back, I would still be interpreting things in my head about what people said, did, or meant. In my untraining process, I learned to listen to the clients better and really hear what things meant for them rather than what I *thought* things meant. I had to learn to stay more curious in my listening and question asking.

Another big unlearning for me (and what I feel is one of the true advanced skills of facilitating the EAGALA Model) is how to use this listening process to ask the minimal but salient questions that deepen the client's process. I was already good at asking questions, but learning how to ask only a few questions that still deepen the process continues to be one of the greatest challenges for me professionally.

Another area of unlearning occurred around the horses. Because I had no real horse knowledge, I would ask my ES partner questions about what she thought the horses were doing during sessions. I wanted to understand the horses better, but this question asking would then take me away from observing the client's interactions with the horses. In the beginning my lack of horse knowledge also impacted my own comfort level in the arena. When there was more activity from the horses, it was harder to be present with the client because of my own fears.

> I had to learn to be open to experience and explore some of my own stuff that I brought to sessions and be willing to work on that stuff to be a better facilitator. The EAGALA Model forces you to deal with it head on.

The equine specialist likewise must relearn what it means to work with a horse in this context. Mounted work and a directive approach are what many horse professionals know. It is challenging working from the ground—challenging for most horse professionals to allow horses this kind of freedom and to remove their intervention and acknowledge the validity of horses' reactions around clients. Although many horsemanship paths have now enriched our understanding of the potential of working with horses at liberty, EAGALA acknowledges this work may not be the right path for some horse people.

When embarking on their EAGALA journey, the discerning horse person may recognize many similarities to his or her former equestrian work. Skilled facilitation as an ES requires developing timing, balance, and feel during the sessions, just as it does working with horses. Concepts such as drive and draw, pressure and release, and approach and retreat can have their place in the arena with both humans and horses. Developing a sensibility for the progression of sessions across the treatment plan and for individual session timing can have a similar feel to working with and training horses over the course of time.

But even with these parallel concepts, many inexperienced equine specialists struggle when it comes to equine-assisted work. EAGALA untraining asks the ES to release deeply ingrained mind-sets—and the limiting perspectives they often come with—to embrace a new approach. Over the years EAGALA trainers have identified several typical areas of untraining equine specialists might need:

- Releasing the desire to direct clients in how to work with the horses.
- Subconsciously directing or teaching clients to do things that are typical horsemanship skills (e.g., handing them a halter and rope

to lead a horse—giving the message that these tools are required to lead a horse).

- Acknowledging that horses and "natural horse behaviors" can have meaning and significance for the clients. Behaviors an ES may take for granted or typically brush off every day may hold deep meaning for the clients.
- Recognizing the value of noticing the smallest horse SPUD. We'll have examples of this in coming chapters.
- Being able to go into the client's perspective of what the horse means to him or her—that is, not looking at the horses as horses but going with the client into the metaphoric world and what the horses become in that story.

Truly skilled EAGALA facilitators maintain a curious mind-set during their client sessions—always willing to learn, always open to things they might never have seen or experienced with horses in the past. Becoming a horse person is a never-ending, evolving process, and the EAGALA Model involves working with horses in a very different way. The horse interacts and, in many ways, actually *guides* clients in the process of change and growth.

If an ES in training is insistent on his or her methods or insistent on helping clients "get it right," the specialist may not adapt well to the EAGALA Model. The EAGALA training is not about questioning an ES on his or her horse expertise but rather asking the specialist to use it in a different way. The horse person who is rigid in his or her belief about how horses should be handled and what should be allowed in an EAGALA session is not ideal for this model. The EAGALA ES accesses a different kind of knowledge and learning when it comes to working with horses.

This is the story about my transition from a traditional horse trainer to an equine specialist working within the EAGALA Model. In 2001, I was working at a residential treatment facility and challenged with starting an equine program. Keep in mind previous people at this facility had already failed at this task, and I was determined to prove that it could be done. So I went online and did some research into equine programs and stumbled across EAGALA.

Some background here: I had spent my horsemanship career training Arabian horses, and I knew all about the prejudices and politics in the horse world. People like a certain breed, while they bash other breeds. People have strong opinions, philosophies, training methods, and riding disciplines.

My comfort level when I first started this work entailed working with a client mounted on a horse in a sixty-foot round pen with a halter and lead rope. I knew how to develop people and horses for the show ring and how to win.

So when I went to my first EAGALA training, I came away at the end of three days mad and upset. It felt like they spent the whole weekend telling me how my knowledge, my experience, and what I'd done with horses my whole career were wrong.

In that first training, I remember watching a fellow student volunteer to ground tie the horse. Now, in horsemanship language, ground tying a horse looks a certain way: you have the horse, you drop the reins or lead rope, and the horse stays put. Simple. It was a basic, disciplined training principle of traditional horsemanship.

So when they asked this woman to go out and "ground tie" a horse, I had a very clear idea of what it was supposed to look like. But instead, the student went out, stood next to the horse, and kept ahold of the lead rope. They asked her to walk around the horse and do it as many times as she would like, at whatever distance she liked. She started walking around the horse, but as she walked, she *still had ahold of the lead rope*, so the horse, quite naturally, also turned around with her. She couldn't seem to grasp the idea of letting go of the lead rope so that the horse could stand still.

I watched this from outside of the arena, and I felt myself start to breathe hard. I began pacing back and forth. I was getting mad, thinking about how she was confusing this poor horse. Why do they not teach her how? Why don't they tell her what to do? Every time she went around the horse, she turned it around. After what felt like hours (but was probably about six minutes), I finally climbed the fence, walked up to the horse, and took the lead rope out of her hand. "You're confusing this horse. You need to sit down," I said, snapping my fingers and pointing at her. "Watch how it's done."

I then proceeded to ground tie the horse until he was standing absolutely still. His ears were forward, and his attention was totally on me. I felt pretty satisfied I had trained the horse to do what he was supposed to do.

All of a sudden, the woman jumped up. "This happens to me all the time! This is exactly how everybody treats me. They don't let me figure it out on my own. I didn't *want* to let go of the horse. I wanted to maintain a connection."

Looking back now, I can kind of laugh and make fun of myself. But back then, at that time in my life, I was a recently separated single dad with sole custody of my daughter. I was in the middle of a career change after losing my horse business, and I was looking for a new home. Everything in my life was uncertain. The one certain thing I carried into that training was my belief in my horsemanship skills.

I came to the EAGALA training so I could get an equine program running in a residential setting, *not* to have my skills questioned or challenged. At that point my horsemanship skills were my identity, the only thing I had control of that someone hadn't taken away from me.

As I stood in the arena that day, puffed up after displaying my considerable horsemanship knowledge, the session suddenly turned into Mark being client number one. But I didn't recognize it as such. I didn't recognize how I took matters out of the client's hands and turned the session into something else. In fact, I left that first training quite upset and then proceeded to come back five more times before the light bulb finally went off.

My horsemanship skills weren't being challenged; I wasn't being told they were wrong. I was being asked to use my experience and horse knowledge in a different way. Once this made sense, I got hungry and went to many, many more trainings. And I'm still continuing on this journey. I still use my horsemanship knowledge every day, every second I'm in the arena. I'm just using it in a more distinctive but subtle way.

As a horse trainer instructing or helping people with their horses, we want to shape people to our beliefs, to respect our knowledge, to do it our way. In contrast, the EAGALA Model equine specialist wants clients to do it for themselves.

"Be yourself" is a really different way to look at it versus "be like me." We want people to do things the way we do things; that's comfortable for us. Allowing people to be themselves can be uncomfortable.

This isn't the only example I have in my journey. There are many, many instances where these two worlds collided for me. A lot of horse people carry ego into the arena. We want to be successful, whether we're training show horses or racehorses or doing natural horsemanship. We want our horses to perform and do the best they can. In the EAGALA Model, allowing people—and the horses—to be themselves may be awkward; it's not easy to look at. You really have to learn to trust the process.

In the last fifteen years, my threshold for these things has broadened, and I'm really thankful. I've probably missed a lot of opportunities. The biggest thing is to let go and realize the solution is already in the arena: it's the horse; it's the client; it's the process!

The EAGALA Model may be a big shift for many mental health professionals and horse people alike. Repurposing years of skill building and knowledge is not easy. Even harder is allowing clients, most of whom have never even been around a horse, to approach and work with horses in a totally novel way from how we were trained as "right" or "proper."

Key Two: Focus on the Ground

> *The horse is a great equalizer…he takes*
> *you for how you make him feel.*
> —BUCK BRANNAMAN

When the concept of EAP/EAL was first formed, working with mounted clients was somewhat of a given; therapeutic riding and hippotherapy modalities had been working with mounted-client populations for years. Working from the ground was more novel. As EAGALA's psychotherapy-specific focus grew, however, working with horses from the ground became a primary process.

Ground-based sessions give horses in a session greater ability to access their natural instincts and inclinations and greater freedom to react naturally and be themselves. Facilitators discovered that these additional equine dynamics, genuinely acknowledged and fluidly managed, yield vast amounts of rich data for the client's self-discovery. As the EAGALA Model took shape, working from the ground seemed to yield everything that was needed and more.

In contrast, putting clients in the saddle introduced a whole new set of dynamics, putting the focus on skills necessary to control the horse safely.

Mounted work required instruction and added risk. Most of all, it added another layer of complexity between the client and his or her story.

Working from the ground further removed the facilitators' ability to influence or control the situation, allowing clients more access to their own solutions. On the ground, the relationship and power dynamic to the horse changed.

In the EAGALA Model, the horse is accorded full status as a professional. Indeed, the most powerful moments of any given session come from the horses and the questions they evoke. Accepting the validity of this can be a struggle for both mental health professionals and equine specialists, but the fact is, horses under saddle simply cannot be themselves as freely. Ground-based interaction with humans allows the horses to have the same choices we have. This is what we want: to give horses the ability to make decisions and respond, to show us what's happening by providing their feedback. To do this, they need to access innate prey-animal behavior without restriction.

A ground-based model helps prevent sessions from becoming unbalanced or turning into either horsemanship lessons or talk therapy in which a horse is merely present.[7] There is a practical aspect to ground-based sessions as well. Though we all know incidents can still happen, unmounted interaction with horses is statistically safer than mounted interaction. No instructions are needed to keep clients safe in the saddle. For those in the public who consider riding a recreational activity, unmounted work helps to enhance the perception that EAGALA's intent is different from recreational activity and from other models.

Key Three: Ethics

Over and over again, the code of ethics is the element that gives the EAGALA Model credibility in the therapeutic world. Elevating our ethical standards gives weight to the work we do.

We work with clients at a vulnerable time in their lives. In working with horses in both EAP and EAL, our clients' vulnerabilities tend to become easily exposed. Therefore, it is our utmost duty to provide the highest quality of care in supporting the overall health and well-being of both our clients and horses, and maintain the highest level of professionalism in our practice and work.

The components of our ethical standard include:[8]

- Each member of the EAGALA team is responsible for the professional status of the team in its entirety. The ES must demonstrate sufficient equine experience and background in horse behavior and psychology, and adhere to ethical codes addressing equine

---

7 EAGALA, *Fundamentals of the EAGALA Model*, 23.
8 EAGALA, *Fundamentals of the EAGALA Model*, 27–31.

welfare and responsible care.[9] The MH must adhere to the professional standards, credentialing, and ethical guidelines of his or her respective governing bodies, states, and countries.

- Both members of the team must understand the responsibilities, ethics, and legal issues of providing therapy to people and avoid misrepresentation of the EAGALA Model, level of professional credentials and qualifications, or operating outside their areas of expertise.

- The EAGALA team must adhere to professional standards of informed consent, documentation, and confidentiality. At all times clients should be aware of the nature, purpose, goals, techniques, and limitations of the services provided, in addition to their rights of confidentiality. Best-practice considerations also include avoiding misinterpretation, miscommunication, and role confusion. Practitioners must be aware of the influential position they maintain with clients, avoiding dual relationships and creating the necessary boundaries to protect both clients and the integrity of the program.

- The horse is regarded as a professional, allowed to participate with respect, integrity, independence, and self-care, no matter its breed or size. In responding freely to human clients, the horse's responses are recognized as appropriate and powerful feedback within the therapy relationship.

- Within the industry, EAGALA professionals carry the responsibility of acting in a supportive and ethical manner toward fellow professionals to help elevate the field of EAP as a whole. This includes sharing areas of expertise and referring to programs of specialized expertise when necessary.

- In practicing the EAGALA Model, we always choose specific horse activities and interventions with deliberate considerations that include addressing specific treatment goals, providing reasons behind specific interventions, and working within the EAGALA standards.

---

9 Many countries have now adopted ethical codes for horse welfare. EAGALA formally endorses the American Horse Council's Welfare Code of Practice, which serves as an official part of EAGALA's standards and ethics. Learn more at www.horsecouncil.org/national-welfare-code.

The EAGALA framework is designed to support clients in their work. It's also designed to give facilitating teams the structure they need to handle any situation that may come their way. Not every case ends on a high note; without all the pieces of the model, many situations have the potential to pull the EAGALA team off balance and into crisis.

This story is called "I Am Resolved." It's not one of my feel-good stories, but it's an important one because it focuses on some of the challenges we face following the EAGALA ethics in our role as facilitators. It's also a story about being careful not to take on the client's story.

We were working with a weekly group of adolescent males on a range of different psychoeducational goals, everything from boundaries to relationships and other things. One of the young men in the group had been recently hospitalized for suicidal ideation and attempt. The therapist had told us what was going on, so we all knew the situation.

When the group came on this day, we checked in to see how everybody was doing. One particular young man—I'll call him Johnny—had been a current member of the group for several months, but today he was very quiet.

We gave the group instructions to go out and divide the horses up, with an equal number of people and horses both sides of the arena. We then asked them to move from one end of the arena to the other in their assigned horse-human groups. Initially there was lots of activity, and some of the horses were moving very fast. We noticed Johnny kept moving away from the group, so we checked in, "Hey, Johnny, we notice that you're moving away from the horses and people."

He said, "Yeah, too much going on."

Then things shifted. Johnny lay down in the middle of the arena and put his hands on his chest. He then got back up and proceeded to put down three buckets. He lay across the buckets and crossed his arms.

We asked, "Johnny, what's happening?"

He responded, "I am resolved."

Meanwhile, the horses—two minis, another little pony named Queen—and Jack, my donkey, began moving again. Jack the donkey then proceeded to jump completely over Johnny as he lay there.

We checked in again. "Johnny, what's going on?"

Again he said, "I'm fine. I'm all right. I am resolved."

The rest of the group continued working on their activity, and the horses seemed to move faster and in more directions. We stopped several times to check in on what was happening. What was so unique, even eerie, was that the group seemed unaware of Johnny lying right in the middle of all the movement and activity. We checked in with the group, and not one mentioned Johnny, who was still lying in the middle of the arena on the buckets. So we decided to ask directly about it. "What's happening over there, where there's one person lying down in the middle of the space and where a horse had jumped right over him?"

Their response was that he was being "covered," as in "protected," by the horses. They thought that the horse jumping over Johnny was trying to protect him. Johnny himself never responded to their remarks.

At this point, the therapist and the other staff from the residential setting formed a huddle away from the group. "Johnny's using the word 'resolved,' and he looks like he's lying in a casket. This just doesn't feel right. It's like he isn't even there."

We decided the session had reached its peak. When we circled up, Johnny didn't really check in except for asking to say good-bye to a horse that wasn't in the arena. At this point, our staff, the residential staff, and primary therapist all came together again. Everyone confirmed that it looked like Johnny was showing signs of suicidal ideation. So before they left, my EAGALA team documented that Johnny appeared to be putting himself in harm's way and at risk. We documented his statement that he "was resolved" when asked a question. In light of his hospitalization the prior week, we noted our concerns that he had at least suicidal ideations, if not plans. He exhibited all the potential to cause harm if not addressed.

The residential staff did a suicide assessment and created a safety plan for going back to the residential house, and the group left. Sure enough, forty minutes after going back to the residential setting, Johnny went to the bathroom and attempted to hang himself in the shower.

It turns out that when the staff arrived at the group home, they didn't put him on suicide watch or anything. The primary therapist went home; the residential staff left. Within an hour Johnny obtained a belt, went into the bathroom, and hanged himself and was hanging for twenty minutes. Luckily, he survived.

I can't explain why the residential staff didn't follow through, but when we heard the news the next morning, our team was really impacted. As we gathered for session, one ES reacted by unloading on everyone and blaming the EAGALA session for being too much for Johnny. But the opposite was true: the session was what very clearly brought Johnny's situation to the forefront. It revealed his suicidal ideation in front of his primary therapist and members of the residential team who were in the arena and part of the conversation.

As it turns out, the kid was going to be all right. But this was really tough learning for us as a team. We implemented a higher level of care at this point to help the whole team handle the situation. But I don't know that this ES is ever going to get past what happened. We debriefed and referred her to a therapist. She even talked to the therapist who was there, but so far she's been unsuccessful at processing her guilt and blame and getting past what happened.

As for my organization, we observed and reported what we knew to be true. We followed procedure and worked with the residential team to note his behavior. We helped form a plan to get Johnny safely back to the house. Ultimately what happened at the residential center once Johnny returned was beyond our control and responsibility. We were all shaken, but we had to draw a clear line and accept that we did our job—the session revealed the depth of the situation.

There are lots of things all professionals have to take into consideration when doing therapeutic work. You need to be OK with handling *all* the possible outcomes, even very serious outcomes like this. Things can go wrong despite our best efforts, but once you take on guilt and blame for it, it's hard to get off. You "can't get any on ya," as the saying goes. You have to know how to keep perspective.

Not all your client sessions are going to feel good or end well, and some situations are going to be really tough. In the EAGALA Model, we believe people do not change if they're comfortable. In life, if everything were comfortable, we would never make changes for the better. I believe that wholeheartedly and take that with me in a lot of things I do.

The sobering outcome of this case reflects the importance of team members being clear in their personal balance, their procedures, and their contractual arrangements and boundaries in carrying out therapeutic work. It also illustrates the importance of EAGALA's professional standards, of having an MH present within the team even within a learning or psycho-education context, and how we work with third parties in handling client situations and processing all situations, especially those with potentially serious and at-risk outcomes.

Key Four: Solution Oriented

As our client cases point out again and again, the EAGALA Model operates under the theory that clients always have the best solution. We create the setting that allows clients to find their own way. We work as a team to get out of their way.

We do not offer solutions, nor do we instruct the clients in how to interact with horses. We encourage them to develop their own methods, their own interpretations, and their own form of problem solving. This in turn enables them to take these new skills and apply them in the real world. As the EAGALA manual states, the goal is for clients to *get* better, not just *feel* better.

Allowing clients freedom to succeed or fail is critical to a solution-oriented process. But as soon as facilitators begin to intervene in the client process, any number of things can happen: The client might back off and allow the therapist to lead the process. Clients may abandon their own discovery to assume the facilitator's point of view. They may also reenact or engage their own default relationship patterns, either opposing the facilitator or subsuming the facilitator's presumed "solution." Meanwhile, deeper and more significant possibilities remain undiscovered and undeveloped. As one EAGALA article noted, when "helping" professionals just can't stop helping, it becomes a detriment to clients.

The consequences of disallowing clients their struggles are immense. In an EAGALA session, we tell the client it is the journey that is important. If we "help," that vital message becomes just one more lie, since it was clearly important to someone that the client find the "answer." In the rush to help the client feel successful, clues to the client's way of approaching conflict or challenge are ignored or minimized. As a result, much therapeutic time is wasted, and the mixed messages can stall or reverse progress.[10]

Ultimately the client needs to learn to feel good without the horses, to go beyond the session and become more effective in solving his or her own challenges. In generating their own solution, what clients accomplish in session becomes their solutions in life.

This requires the facilitating team to operate free of expectations at all times, to stand back and allow clients to struggle while we hold them in their own potential. We don't want to block that process, physically or verbally. Even when it pushes our boundaries and the boundaries of the EAGALA Model, we need to stand in the perspective that clients have the best solutions when given the opportunity to discover them.

This story is called "I Can See Clearly Now," and it's a story of how one client-led solution took shape for us. It's also an example of how a client's own metaphor in the EAGALA Model can sometimes trump our definition of what's "proper" in the traditional horse world.

We had a young family come in as an adjunct part of an intensive in-home therapy program. The daughter was the identified client, but it was a family-based session. These folks had been out a couple of times, and the parents were fairly combative with each other verbally. If one would say, "The sky was blue," the other one would say, "No, it's pink," just out of spite.

We asked the family to go into the arena and create a path from the props that would represent where they wanted their family to be—to start where it was now and create a "road map" to their ideal family.

10 Beth Avolio, "Strategies to Resist the Assist," *EAGALA in Practice* 4 no. 1 (2011): 22.

So they started working and trying to build this path, and the banter started right up. If Dad said, "Let's do this," then Mom said, "Heck no."

Two of the four horses were very involved in what was going on. If the parents set up a pole or a barrel, they would go knock it over. This went on for about twenty minutes, and then we realized the other two horses were pretty much nonexistent in this dynamic—not anywhere close to the couple and at first seemingly out of sight. We also realized the daughter, Susan, was just as nonexistent.

We looked around and saw Mr. Cool, one of our larger horses, standing against the back rail of the arena with our miniature donkey Jack standing right beside him. And there, sitting on *top* of Mr. Cool, was Susan. How she got there was a mystery. We stopped the session; Mom and Dad were still bickering in the middle of the arena, and the two horses were still knocking things over.

We asked, "Hey, guys, we're just kind of wondering: where's Susan?"

The parents looked around. Mom asked, "Did she leave the arena?" Finally, they saw her and immediately started pointing fingers. "Oh my God, who let her on that horse? There's nobody holding that horse. Who did this?"

We broke in. "Well, we're wondering how often this happens—where Susan is up somewhere, out of sight."

This led to a discussion where Dad admitted, "She's never in my sight."

The mother also conceded that they got so wound up in their own stuff that they often forgot about Susan and what Susan needed and wanted. "How did you get her up there without us seeing?" asked Mom.

We said, "We didn't put her up there."

So we asked Susan to get off. She threw her right leg over the horse's neck and then proceeded to lower herself down from Mr. Cool's back to Jack's back, and then down to the ground. Both horses stood completely still while she did this. So now we knew exactly how she got on.

We asked her, "Susan, what did you notice while you were sitting up a little higher?"

She said, "Everybody's always fighting."

I asked, "What did you notice that the horses were doing?"

She said, "Well, these two were with my mom and dad, tearing each other down just like at home. I was over here with my grandparents."

Through the following sessions, Susan was able to admit she preferred being with her grandparents. She wanted to live with them because they provided the security and stuff that she wanted and needed. Her mom and dad were so focused on themselves that she was never noticed.

So in "I Can See Clearly Now," we have an illustration of how a client did what she needed to do. She put herself up in a place that was literally as high and as far away from her parents as she could get. The horses cooperated with her fully. Her parents were able to see exactly how their actions affected their daughter, pushing her to take things into her own hands. Although it really stretched the limits of safety in our minds, in Susan's mind, being on the horse's back was a safe place, with Mr. Cool and Jack taking care of her just like her grandparents do.

Putting the Pieces Together

In the EAGALA Model, what matters is the meaning the client puts on the experience. The components of the model help us to accomplish those ends and create the ideal environment for exploration, problem solving, and discovery.

Learning to create and facilitate that process is where the true art exists. The tools we use to help clients reach this place are not necessarily the tools we were originally taught to use as either mental health or equine professionals. So how do we, as professionals from two distinct fields, train to unite as a single team and fulfill the unique requirements of EAGALA? How do we rewire our mind-sets to explore a client's thoughts, beliefs, and behaviors through the horse?

This will be the focus of our next two chapters.

CHAPTER 4

The EAGALA Process

Now we have the basic pieces to begin equine-assisted psycho-therapy: the horse, the arena, and the structure of the EAGALA Model. Our intake is complete, and the treatment goals are clear. Our client has stepped into the arena with the horses.

So now what? How does the team actually put the EAGALA process into action?

Earlier we introduced the EAGALA observational framework, called SPUD'S, a methodology used by the team to track the activity and re-sponses of both horse and client, although the primary focus is on the horses and symbols. As a client session progresses, the first four SPUD'S criteria allow the team to focus, pinpoint, and define moments of sig-nificance. The treatment team then takes these observations and reflects them back to the client in the form of question asking, observational state-ments, metaphors, and invitations for clients to share their story. The four SPUD'S, combined with these two actions—observing and reflecting—form the backbone of session execution.

The SPUD'S framework includes four criteria: Shifts, Patterns, Unique aspects, and Discrepancies. The model has evolved over the years, but its basic structure and intention remain the same: to make observations free of interpretation. In any given case, noted SPUD'S moments may be incredibly subtle or obvious and overt. The significance of the moment may be completely immaterial to the size of the moment; something we understand as small may carry immense meaning to the client.

S: Shifts

Shifts in an EAGALA session pertain to any physical or behavioral change in the horses, other symbols, or the humans. Examples of Shifts: The horses were together, but now they're apart. They were standing still, but now they are moving. The gate was open, and then it was closed. The client was outside along the wall but is now standing in the center of the arena. Every Shift in session, no matter how small, correlates to *movement*. Tracking movement is essential because *movement* indicates *change*. And change, in one form or another, is the global objective for both client and team. Shift by Shift, bit by bit, the client moves further from whatever state has him or her mired or stuck in place.

P: Patterns

In the same way that Shifts indicate movement, Patterns that show up during client sessions usually indicate deeper meaning behind the client's behavior. A Pattern is indicated when the same behavior occurs three or more times. With the primary focus being on observations of horses and other symbols in the environment, some pattern examples might be the horses moving in circles several times, a barrel being knocked over by a horse at least three times, or two horses staying near each other consistently through the session.

U: Unique Aspects

Anything that is out of the ordinary for your horse or human counts as a Unique aspect, both within their general behavior as horses or humans and within their specific personalities. This is where knowing your herd of horses really counts; recognizing that a moment is Unique or out of character requires first knowing what is normal. The key to tracking Unique aspects in a session is not the moment in and of itself; it's also being sure to note it within the context or backdrop of the entire arena at that moment. Perhaps it's unusual for that mare to kick out or for that horse to move away from his herd members. In chapter 3, Susan climbing on small Jack to get on top of tall Mr. Cool, and the horses' complete stillness in that process, was a unique moment that had significance for that client and family.

D: Discrepancies

Discrepancies are moments of incongruence noted in the human client, when the client says one thing but his or her nonverbal actions say another. Noting a Discrepancy is key to helping clients move from pre-awareness to awareness. Facilitators are continuously comparing verbal to nonverbal. Do they match? In helping clients learn to become aware of situations in which their external actions fail to match their words, clients can move themselves past the blocks, defense mechanisms, and self-talk that create incongruence. By becoming aware, they can self-adjust to bring verbal and nonverbal communication together to create change.

Putting It Together: The Art of Observation and Reflection

The SPUD'S observational process is ongoing through the client session. However, it's at the point of using a SPUD moment that the facilitator's skill level, training, and personal awareness come to the forefront. The crux of the EAGALA Model—and its success—often hinge on how we state or reflect a session SPUD back to the client.

The technique and manner of a facilitator's reflection can mean the difference between having a moment of change put upon the client through our external influence or setting up the observation in a way that allows the *client* to uncover personally the significance, opportunity, or solution that comes from any given SPUD. EAGALA's solution-oriented model recognizes that a client's most powerful learning comes from his or her own discovery. The client needs to change from his or her *own* direction. How we set up our SPUD'S reflection is key.

For every EAGALA professional, being effective with SPUD'S moments comes from understanding that, in the SPUD'S process, our only job is to reflect the SPUD back to the client. The significance of the SPUD, or how it may serve the client, is not our job to interpret. The facilitator should not attempt to understand the meaning behind it or presume to judge a SPUD by its shape or size; what appears minor to us can have major meaning to the client.

Achieving this clear distinction is an ongoing discipline. One tool utilized in EAGALA training is called "keeping language clean," which helps facilitators minimize the influence of their interpretation on a SPUD. Being "clean" helps break down an observation into its most elemental parts so that interpretation and opinion are eliminated as much as possible. The smallest nuance in an observation matters. For example, to say, "The horse *pushed* you forward" can imply a manner or meaning in the horse's action that influences the client's response. To say instead, "The horse put his nose on your chest, and you moved forward" removes that implication, leaving room for the client to put his or her own meaning into it. A client may not realize a horse's action would be considered rude or pushy by a traditional horse person; in the client's eyes, it may appear as *helpful* or *protective* or any number of other things. Our traditional interpretation may block that response.

No matter how an observation is reflected back to the client, skilled facilitators always work to consciously keep their language clean by removing all interpretation and opinion from that reflection, whether implied or overt.

Putting It Together

The story below illustrates how SPUD'S can take shape in a client session. Pay attention to how a singular, Unique aspect of the horses' behavior becomes a Pattern for this client. You'll also see aspects of Shifts, Discrepancy, and clean facilitation here too.

"Alice" was a seventeen-year-old international client, here in the United States for a short period of intense individual sessions. Back home, she had been the top female golfer in her age group for eight years and had won two national titles in dance. Fourteen months prior to our sessions, all of that stopped abruptly. She went from dancing four to five times a week and golfing daily to partying really hard and getting out of control. We were told her mom did not know where she was most of the time. She was drinking and partying and was verbally abusive with no respect for herself or others.

In our first session, Alice walked in stating she hated therapy. She did very little moving during the session and whined and complained a lot. When she finally approached one horse and petted him, he turned, opened his mouth, and put his teeth on her. We checked in, but she didn't want to talk about it or anything else. We just observed, letting her have her moment without applying too much pressure by asking questions.

The next day we went into the arena and another horse, named Fashion, walked straight up and did the same thing. This became the progression of every session we had: she got bitten every day by a different horse. The horse would walk up with no hesitation about it, put its teeth on her, and leave. None of the other horses would come up. It was as if someone needed to do it. When it was done, it was done.

We obviously didn't want her to keep getting bitten, but we went with it, because it was so Unique that these horses were doing this behavior and because of her odd reaction to it. Despite what the horses were doing, *not once* did she do anything about it. She didn't move. She didn't try to hide behind us. She just took the bite.

The therapist and I created a session to explore this dynamic. It was evident that there were boundary issues happening, along with something else we couldn't define. We asked Alice to create a space representing something she considered hers, something she would be willing to protect. She created a square box, which she called her life. Then she put buckets of feed inside the box. In addition to being valued by the horses, these buckets also represented the things she valued, which included her mom, her friends, and her stuff. We asked her to protect those things she valued from the horses.

Once we invited her to protect what she valued, she cried out, "I don't want to be here. This is awful!" As she said that, the horses began moving toward the box, where had she placed all of the buckets of feed on top of each other. Alice immediately stuck her arm out. The first horse to approach began licking her all over— her arms, her neck, her shirt. Then he put his teeth on her and held on. A second horse came over, and Alice stuck her *other* arm out. This horse also licked her and licked her before taking her arm in his mouth.

So here we had a girl, charged with protecting things she cared about, sticking her arms out voluntarily so that two horses could bite her and hold on. The MH and I expressed our shock with one another; we couldn't believe what we were seeing. To the client, we put out a clean observation: "We noticed that two horses have two arms in their mouths."

She said, "Yes, I'm protecting my stuff."

Sure enough, the hay and grain—the things she valued— didn't get a nibble. The horses didn't even try to eat any of the hay and grain she was protecting. We responded, "OK, Alice, we're wondering if there are things in your life that, in order to protect them, you offer yourself instead."

This prompted quite a response: she ran out of the arena screaming, "I don't want to be here!"

A few minutes later, she came back in and opened up. Fourteen months earlier, her mom had taken in a nineteen-year-old boarder. He started buying her alcohol and partying, and after a period of time had sex with her while she was under the influence. She went to her mom and reported, "Mom, this happened. I'm scared. I don't know what to do."

Mom's response? "We need the money. Keep your mouth shut."

You can imagine what that was like, what it did to that kid to have her mom put that responsibility on her. From that day forward, her old life stopped. She stopped playing golf and dancing.

After Alice disclosed this in the EAGALA session, she started making some real changes in her behavior and attitude, including being much more open and willing with the therapy process. She returned home at the completion of the designated trip, and in that first year, she stayed in almost daily contact with us, giving updates about her life. She is doing really well, making changes and healthy choices. As for her mom, the day after Alice arrived back home, they started going to family therapy and are doing well.

SPUD'S aside, no doubt this story trips a lot of triggers for people. No one wants their clients to get bitten, right? As a professional facilitator, instinct probably tells us we are supposed to prevent that. At the same time, the horses in this case displayed very clear SPUD'S by doing something completely Unique, which then became a very visible Pattern. The client's reaction—or lack thereof—was also Unique.

Trusting our horses when a Unique moment occurs brings forth an-other aspect of the EAGALA Model: trusting the process. This trust is a big part of this or any EAGALA session, going beyond our interpretation of "good" or "bad" in judging the horses' actions to trusting that what the horses are doing and saying merits attention. If at any time the fa-cilitators had stopped to direct the client *not* to put her arms out or to make sure she didn't allow the horses to put their mouths on her, it would have blocked the process. Symbolically, offering her arms to the horses "physicalized" what was going on inside of her, something she never spoke about until that moment triggered her to disclose it. Notice the use of the facilitator's clean wording in processing this SPUD: "It appears two horses have two arms in their mouths." Despite being somewhat alarmed by the horses' actions, the facilitators remained neutral in their statements.

This case also highlights monitoring the progression of sessions over the course of a client's treatment plan. In this case, the SPUD'S built to a tipping point of sorts over a period of time. The team's experience and professional instincts told them it was time to focus on the Pattern itself. Their timing was important here, bringing the issue to a peak at just the right time so it propelled the client to open the door on her issue.

Focusing on the SPUD'S helps EAGALA facilitators pay attention to the nonverbals of both horses and clients in session. Sometimes these nonverbal aspects are quite subtle, other times quite outrageous, as in the story below.

This is a story that really brings the concept of SPUD'S and the power of the two-person team together. It also highlights a case where Unique aspects are sometimes lurking in places where we can miss them. It's one I call "Full of Crap."

Have you ever heard of the movie *The Stepford Wives*, where the women were perfect beyond belief? Well, this was a "Stepford family," referred to us by an agency. It was supposed to be therapy for the young teenage daughter; however, the dad refused to let her do therapy without the whole family being part of the session. This insistence by Dad put up a red flag for us right away.

The family arrived, and throughout the whole first session, they were the perfect Stepford family, telling us what they thought we should hear, rather than telling us the whole truth. The whole family acted plastic, with a flat aspect. Their movement around the horses was robotic, really strained and awkward. When we checked in, their answers were very flat. "How was it out there?" we'd ask.

"Fine," they'd respond.

"What happened in the experience?" we'd ask.

"I don't know," was the typical response.

We let things play out and then circled up at the end, where the dad was doing all the talking, and again no one was very forthcoming. We were about to wrap up the session when, bless his heart, my miniature horse, Twister, joined the group. Twister brushed against my leg and then walked over to the dad. He turned around and faced me, backed up to the dad, lifted his tail, and pooped all over the man's shoes.

In the aftermath was complete silence. The Stepford family didn't say a single word. Mother didn't make a sound. Daughter didn't say "Oh, gross!" Dad didn't do anything, not even shake the crap off his shoes.

I opened my mouth to ask the obvious question of what just happened there, but then I looked over at my therapist partner, who shook her head as if to say, "Don't say a word!" I was dying to say something, but I trusted her and shut my mouth. "OK," we said to the family, "see you next week." When Dad walked out, he just stepped out of the pile of poop but didn't shake it off or anything.

After the family left, my MH and I debriefed what had just happened. Twister's actions were so Unique, I was overwhelmingly curious to find out what was going on. But my therapist was the one who looked even deeper, "OK, Twister gave us a SPUD. But them not saying anything was even *more* of a SPUD. What's bigger than the crap on his shoes is the lack of response from the family. Something is going on here, and we can't push it until someone in that family feels emotionally safe enough to speak." I agreed to wait with her until the moment was right.

The next week came, and we did a check-in. The family was still not saying much or responding much verbally. No one mentioned the crap from last week, so we began the session. Afterward, as we were processing, lo and behold, here came Twister. Once again, he turned around, lifted his tail, backed up, and pooped all over Dad's feet.

The MH and I were both shocked Twister did this again—and once again, nobody responded; there was no effect from anybody. My therapist partner gave me *the look*, and once again I bit my tongue to keep from saying anything.

Week three arrived, and the therapist and I discussed that if the Unique incident happened again, which would now make it an official Pattern, we were going to ask about it.

The family went through the motions of the activities. We were nearing the end, and Twister walked out in front of Dad, about twenty feet in front of him this time. He turned around, looked right at him, and raised his tail. This time he was completely exaggerated; he was farting very loudly, passing gas for the whole twenty feet, and moving directly toward Dad, who didn't even move. There was no doubt in my mind—no doubt in *anyone's* mind—about what was getting ready to happen. Twister got in his final position and crapped all over Dad's feet.

Again, silence. I was very excited. I looked at my partner, who gave me a nod, saying *it's time.* I finally made the statement I'd been dying to make: "We noticed that this is the third session in a row where someone has ended up with something on their shoes."

The girl kind of mumbled, and I asked, "Ma'am, is there something you want to share?" This was the first time the girl had actually spoken more than one word in the sessions. She replied, "The horse knows he's full of shit!"

At this point, several things happened at once. Twister went and stood in between the girl and her dad. Dad's face turned completely white. Mom turned around and started walking toward the gate as if she was leaving. The therapist asked, "Can you explain more about him being full of shit?"

The girl pointed to her mom and replied, "She knows."

Mom turned around and yelled, "Keep your mouth shut!"

My horse, Fred, walked to the other side of Mom, cut her off, and literally started pushing her with his head until she was back with the rest of her family.

Once again, my therapist asked, "OK, what does Mom know?"

Mom said, "I know nothing."

The girl replied, "You know what he does to me; you know!" She then disclosed that her father had been sexually abusing her for many years. She felt like her mom was making it possible, leaving her at home with him alone and making it convenient for him to do that.

Things really got serious. Here we were in an arena, with a daughter disclosing sexual victimization by her father with her mother's knowledge. We had to deliver a report right then and there. The sheriff's department came. When the authorities got there, the father admitted to everything and left in handcuffs. The daughter was taken home by an aunt.

The daughter continued in sessions with us for a couple of years after that. Dad was sentenced, pleaded guilty, and was accountable for everything. It's now been seven years, and the mother has yet to contact her daughter or be involved with her. She is still in denial to this day. The father recently committed suicide, which the daughter has been processing.

For me, this case shows the power in the silence and not jumping on everything that a client gives you in the moment. Could we have said something earlier? I don't think that girl would have felt safe enough to say anything the first couple of times. But by waiting, she felt safe enough to be thinking it, and it came out.

We can't always know if a client feels emotionally safe to share that in that first time, so holding on to that SPUD moment can be very powerful. For this girl, perhaps it was powerful acknowledgment for her to see that Twister apparently saw through this whole affair and wasn't content to let the matter drop. Maybe his actions, repeated three times, were her cue that it was valid. "The horse knows what's going on; maybe this time I'm going to say what I need to."

We talk a lot about metaphors in this work. In this story, it would have been tempting to use the SPUD'S presented by the horse to jump to processing and possible metaphors too early. Twister's SPUD was very obvious. But the therapist recognized a second, less-noticeable SPUD— the family's Discrepancy. She also recognized the emotional implications behind it. Discrepancy in the face of such an outrageous act by the horse implied immense weight. Again, the timing of the team's response was important. Waiting for the metaphor to come out naturally was key to the disclosure.

There are multiple dynamics to manage during a client session. We track client-horse interaction with the SPUD'S framework; we monitor our own "Apostrophe S" dynamics, also known as "my stuff," which we will talk about more later; and then we work to skillfully harness an array of observational tools in providing clear, clean reflections back to the client.

Simplicity is the basis of the EAGALA process, but developing the skills to use it effectively is never ending. The treatment team brings its own professional background and is constantly challenged to hone their observational skills and knowledge to distinguish variations in body language, behavior, and nuances during the interaction. While practitioners learn, they are also challenged in their own self-understanding to remain humble and to allow the client to find his or her own way through metaphor to meaning.

This is the journey we'll explore in the next chapter.

CHAPTER 5

Easier Said Than Done:
Introducing the "Apostrophe S"

One significant aspect of EAGALA Model work is its emphasis on the continuous development of the self-awareness skills of its practitioners. This emphasis is necessitated by EAGALA's solution-oriented model, which requires facilitators to develop a different set of processing "muscles" from those developed in their traditional training. To watch a client struggle means working from a different paradigm, one whereby we understand that we cannot presume to go where the client might go in a session. We cannot anticipate what might be significant or where a client may find a solution.

You may have noticed a fifth component of the SPUD'S framework, the "Apostrophe S" that comes at the very end of the SPUD'S acronym. The Apostrophe S is a powerful and elusive dynamic that influences every session. In fact, the Apostrophe S lurks in nearly every case highlighted in this book. We mention it at this point, separate from the rest, because it's the one dynamic that doesn't represent the client or the horse. The Apostrophe S represents the influence of the facilitating team.

People naturally feel compelled to respond to things as they happen in the arena environment. It's also natural for the client's situation to awaken and draw the facilitator's own experience into the session. Apostrophe

S stands for "my stuff": the belief systems, narratives, experiences, and previous training that influences the facilitating team as they navigate each client session. In the mental health world, this is known as counter-transference. The Apostrophe S is naturally present in each session, simply because we're human beings expressing our human nature. It can't be denied, and yet our awareness of how it influences our client sessions should be constantly monitored.

Starting with early "untraining" and throughout any EAGALA facilitator's professional development, the Apostrophe S is given great focus. Because it has more impact on session outcomes than almost any other factor, it requires consistent work to monitor the influence of our Apostrophe S in creating countertransference issues with the client, as it almost did in this case.

Even as an experienced EAGALA trainer, I am still working to observe and learn everything I can to improve my understanding of different concepts, in order to be a better facilitator. While I do my best to be aware of my Apostrophe S in sessions, this is a story about how an issue I thought I'd resolved long ago showed up, triggered me, and took over in a session. I call this story "Between the Parallel Worlds."

We were in an EAGALA training workshop, demonstrating a sample session. A woman who volunteered to serve as our client for the demonstration built an "alley" that represented the journey she had been on in life. She went through and placed objects in the alley that symbolically represented different moments in her life journey. She then chose a horse to accompany her through her life journey. A couple of times, the horse stopped. At one point he stopped, and with his nose, he started tipping things over and knocking everything down.

At the end of it, we checked in. "Is there anything you would like to share about the journey?" The lady started telling a story about her life in a religious cult. She was still having struggles, in fact, because her brother was involved in the cult.

As facilitators we need to be able to read the client and look for the peaks in the session, being careful not to push a client further than what is emotionally safe for her to go, especially in a training environment like this one. So here we were, immersed in this process, and all of a sudden I could feel my face getting red and my heart beating really hard. As the woman was talking and my MH co-facilitator was asking some questions, I decided that we had hit the session's peak. I looked at my partner and mouthed, "OK, this is enough. It's done. Let's stop." However, the woman was still telling her story and was just fine. My partner gave me a "What's wrong with you?" look, which only made me more animated. My body was shaking and becoming more agitated.

At that moment my partner turned around and—in front of more than seventy trainees—looked at me and said, "Wow, Mark,

I'm noticing it looks like you want to stop this session. Yet the client is still freely talking about it. What's going on with you?"

When she said those words—"What's going on with you?"—it hit me like a ton of bricks. I knew what it was: I didn't want to hear any more of the client's story because she was telling *my* story, a story I lived through many years ago.

Back then, my first wife and her family were involved in a religious cult. Her mom actively practiced in it, and at one point the church kidnapped her little brother and hid him in Switzerland. My first wife and I actually started helping people leave the cult and got very involved in extracting members who wanted to leave. It was a very scary time.

This had been a major piece in my life, and, after many years of therapy, I thought I was past it. Yet at that moment, the woman in the arena was replaying an exact scenario that happened in my life almost twenty years ago. All the emotions I lived through came flooding back in the middle of that training, as if I were back in 1992.

To her credit, my MH partner didn't make it a therapy session. As soon as I named it and I claimed it, I was able to move on and share it with the participants of the training. It was a great learning moment for the EAGALA participants, giving our students a very clear picture of how a facilitator's Apostrophe S could impact a session. There was great feedback and discussion around what had happened to me and how my MH handled it as a learning opportunity for the trainees.

What was most interesting, however, is that as soon as I named it, the horse in the session came and lay down behind me. It was as if the horse knew I had become the client.

This incident happened only a couple of years ago. I thought I was well past the situation, but that day it got very intense very quickly. It came right back to life, and at the moment it occurred, I went someplace that wasn't in the best interest of the student/client.

There is a lot of conversation around exceptions in the EAGALA Model, such as, "Do we really need an MH in an equine-assisted learning session or when we're working with corporate teams?" From this and many other experiences I've had, my answer is yes!

Things happen differently in the experiential setting of the arena. The arena is kinetic; the horses evoke powerful things in all the people present, and it can definitely impact us as facilitators too. There has to be someone who can manage what comes up, even in the most benign, corporate EAGALA session. I don't want to ever go in the arena without a mental health professional.

This is also why the EAGALA Model puts so much focus on the Apostrophe S. The facilitator's own issues can come up, even as we grow in experience and awareness. For me, it highlights again the importance of EAGALA's team approach. You don't know what is going to show up in a session. Having that co-facilitator there to help when our Apostrophe S comes up is powerful. It happens to all of us, and isn't about being hard on ourselves; it's about being conscious and alert. No matter how long we do this work, our stuff is going to show up. Even when you think you've dealt with it and wrapped it up really nicely, it can still show up.

I'm much better now at picking up when something's going on with me. I know the pre-awareness signs and how they manifest in my body. My ears and face get hot and red, my heart starts beating really hard, and I get physically agitated.

Apostrophe S responses can get in the way of what's best for the client. Everything about EAGALA's training prepares facilitators to be conscious and aware of where they come from.

The Apostrophe S influences what we see and how we see it, and that in turn influences how and when we intervene. Because it's human nature—our human nature—it's not an absolute, but imperfect at best.

An Apostrophe S can manifest in curious and very subtle ways:

- The structure of the session itself can affect the clients' discoveries. Sometimes in planning the client's session, facilitators can inadvertently create an agenda that leads the client in a specific direction versus setting a more open stage for discovery.
- Our selection of horses for a session can also be overly directive, designed to lead the client to a specific place as we judge appropriate.
- This, then, can set up a situation where we focus on what *didn't* happen and why it didn't happen in a session when our agenda gets altered.
- Personal beliefs that "our way" is better than the client's way can affect the outcome of a session.
- The session can be influenced verbally by, for example, our tone of voice, timing, "helpful" or "instructional" comments, leading comments, commands, choice of words (for example, *would have*, *could have*, or *should have*), and the like.
- The session can be influenced nonverbally through, for example, posture, crossed muscles, where we choose to stand, how we move, and so on.
- An Apostrophe S can manifest as physical symptoms, such as clenched muscles, stomach butterflies, and sweating.
- Using the words *need*, *want*, or *I* are signals of an Apostrophe S.

Skilled EAGALA facilitators consistently work to remove the influence of the Apostrophe S in creating agenda-filled planning, observations, questions, and processing. The better we are at acknowledging the lens of our own Apostrophe S, the better we will be at producing observations that truly allow clients to discover their own solutions.

Accomplishing this is an ongoing process, requiring facilitators to stand back and consistently and honestly acknowledge their own issues, let go of assumptions, and work from a place of genuine belief in the capabilities of our clients and horses. Working from a place of humility (I don't know the answers) and sincere curiosity (what is this for the client?) is key.

Just how much does our Apostrophe S impact our work? You'd be surprised. I have had many stories, but this is one classic case illustrating how my Apostrophe S affected the session and impacted the horse. This story is called "I'm Being Dumped."

We got a call from a caseworker that a young man, "Jason," we had been seeing was in crisis mode and needed to come in and work some things out with the horses. When he got there, we asked him how he was doing, and he said, "Well, I'm being dumped. My parents are reversing the adoption because I've gotten in trouble."

We asked him which horses he wanted to work with, and he selected two horses out of the pasture, a gray mare and a black gelding named Mr. Cool. He moved the horses over to the arena, and we started.

This was a young client who had been doing EAGALA for a while, so when we asked him what he wanted to work on, he knew exactly what he was after. "Well, I'm over here, and I'm really comfortable over here," he said, pointing to a spot in the arena, "but I need to go over there, and that means I need to accept and be prepared for this change that's happening." He took PVC pipe and made a line across the arena and said, "This side, where the horses are, is where I am. I'm happy and comfortable. But I want to move the horses across the pole. That would represent me crossing over to the new situation."

We went into the arena with him, and as soon as he approached the big, black horse, Mr. Cool turned around and kicked out with both hind legs. I was alarmed and thought, *Oh no. What is this about?* So I moved closer, and as I did, the horse turned around, laid his ears back at me, and came after me.

I thought, *Oh no, you don't*, and my horsemanship stuff kicked right in. I got big, moved in to correct him, and the horse chased me completely out of the arena.

Oh boy, was I mad at this horse! It took me a minute or two to recover, and then I rejoined my therapist partner, and we checked back in with the client. "What's going on?"

Jason said, "Well, I'm not happy about this change," and identified himself as the same horse that had just chased me.

The session progressed further, and at one point we happened to move in a bit closer. Mr. Cool laid his ears back and came at me again. Finally, the MH looked at me and said, "Mark, there's something going on with you and the horse. You need to get out of the arena." With that, the MH and I moved just on the other side of the fence to distance ourselves a bit more from what was happening in the space.

We continued to watch the session. Jason kept trying to get the horse to move over the pole, but Mr. Cool was having none of it, maintaining distance from Jason and staying on this side of the PVC pipe—seemingly refusing to move to the other side that represented Jason's transition. When the session ended, we checked in. "What's going on?"

He said, "Well, I'm just not ready." We left it at that for this session.

After the client left, I went to get the horses out of the arena. Mr. Cool came after me yet again, ears back. He turned around and kicked at me. I was stumped. This horse was nineteen years old. I'd had him since he was five months old and knew him like the back of my hand. There was a story here.

At this point in my EAGALA work, I wasn't aware just how much of our stories played out in the arena. All I knew at the moment was I could not approach this horse. My MH, who was eight months pregnant, finally took her scarf off, walked up to the horse, wrapped the scarf around his neck, and walked him back to the pasture. He dropped his head and was completely willing— and she wasn't even a horse person!

When she came back, she asked, "What is your deal? As soon as Jason said that he was being dumped, your face and ears turned beet red."

Well, I was stumped; then it hit me like a ton of bricks, and I realized the connection. I was a single dad, divorced, with sole custody of my daughter. My ex-wife signed full custody of my daughter to me, but then a couple of months later, she challenged me in court for the ownership of two horses. Mr. Cool was one of those horses. At the time I couldn't reconcile this. She gave my daughter to me but then fought me over a horse, seeming to put more value in this horse than her own daughter—or at least that's what I told myself.

She won the horse in court and took him. Three years later she called me asking if I could come get him because she was behind on board and couldn't pay. Once again she dumped on me, and I was expected to clean up her mess. So I went and got the horse, put him in the pasture, and proceeded to take care of him: feeding him, vaccinating him, getting his feet done.

But what I didn't do was take care of him in any other way. I put him in the pasture and ignored him. Before Jason chose him, I had not even used him in session. In essence, after my ex-wife dumped him on me, *I had dumped him too.*

I didn't want to have anything to do with him because he represented a lot that was hard on me. When this client used the word "dumped," it tripped my trigger, and my whole body responded. Once I realized this, I started my own work to do what I needed to be OK with the horse and my own stuff—stuff that had been buried for six or seven years.

A simple phrase brought it all to the forefront. You never know when your stuff is going to come up. But the team approach helped me become aware. Both Mr. Cool and my MH moved me from pre-awareness to awareness of what was going on and how it impacted the session.

Mr. Cool is now my horse, and our relationship is much different than it was several years ago. In this case, he really called me out and confronted me. He was more aware than I was.

As for Jason, some good stuff came out of our sessions. He came back and worked with Mr. Cool some more and got to a better place with his situation.

A key concept in the solution-oriented model is this: the only way to create the client's path to a solution is to keep the focus on the client's story. Our job is to support the direction and his or her process while holding emotional and physical space for whatever comes forth.

To do this, facilitators need to learn how to recognize where their influence might intersect with the client's progression. For most facilitators, this is an ongoing development process, session by session and day by day. It is natural for facilitators to come to the profession with a desire to help and, like our clients, to have a need or desire to put meaning on the world. We naturally bring our personal stories and Apostrophe S's into the session. But the intersection of our desire to help, combined with our Apostrophe S, will inadvertently create barriers to client success in the solution-oriented aspect of the model.

The Art of Letting Go

The ability of the horses to influence and provoke change in human clients is the crux of the EAGALA Model. A key aspect of EAGALA

Model training involves teaching facilitators to let go of control, to allow this interaction to take place. Human facilitators new to the EAGALA process are often challenged in letting go of control and allowing horses the freedom to interact. This requires facilitators to develop a combination of openness, humility, and curiosity in their approach to sessions.

It also requires identifying and removing facilitator-based agendas from their influence in directing the session progression and in subsequent client processing. Letting go of control helps facilitators allow clients to explore and grow. It creates a setting in which the client's experience and point of view are validated, no matter what shape they take.

One very nuanced example of an Apostrophe S showed up in the case of the *Groundhog Day* Kid, where the "catch and halter" horsemanship language was actually part of the ES's Apostrophe S. "Catch and halter" is common lexicon in the world view of an ES, and it is easy to move unconsciously into placing that world view on our clients. The EAGALA Model is not about horsemanship but about the client's world view being expressed symbolically through the horses and space. Asking a client to "catch and halter" to start a relationship has some potential symbolic connotations about relationships that may not fit well for the client's life story. It is easy for the treatment team to start making assumptions about what the process needs to look like when we use lexicon that comes from our commonly used horsemanship language.

One way of moving beyond this type of Apostrophe S is for facilitators to be more deliberate with the words they use and to understand how those words can relate to the client's needs and life story. It involves really listening to our clients and using their words as our language. In this *Groundhog Day* example, the client was preparing to transition from a correctional institution to the "real world," so an example of what we might invite could be to introduce himself and get to know the world that is here, especially in view of the circumstance that this was the client's first time off the campus since his placement. This language potentially has more immediate relevance and meaning for the client than "go catch and halter a horse." However, the beauty of experiential work is that whatever happens becomes part of the story, and we use it, including our Apostrophe S, just like the way the halter symbolically became "shackling" by this client, something he didn't want to see happen to anyone, including the horses.

Another aspect of this Apostrophe S is recognizing when we have made decisions for our clients instead of providing the space for them to make their own choices. Directing the client to use a halter, for example, *had made a decision for the client*. While there are times to be directive in this way, for the most part we really want to provide a space for our clients to make their own choices about what the process looks like and what tools they use or don't use. It requires keeping that language boundary even cleaner.

Whether ES or MH, the experience we bring to EAGALA Model work is still very important in providing credible and knowledgeable facilitation to the field. However, our job is to also be exceedingly aware of how we assert ourselves—and our preconceived ideas, ingrained beliefs, and "Apostrophe S"—into the client experience. While our experience serves as the backdrop to our work, our bigger job is to trust the process and allow the horses' interactions in the present moment to be the real guide in creating change for our clients.

PART III

Refinement: The Process at Work

CHAPTER 6

Trusting the Process

I f you look hard enough, you'll see almost every case in this book is about trusting the horse-client relationship process once we set things in motion. These examples illustrate the typical journey of the human facilitator in the EAGALA Model and how trusting the process is typically a lesson that needs to be learned over and over again. Amazing things can happen when horses interact with clients. The more we learn to let go and allow the process to unfold, the better it works.

The horse is key to everything. Trust in the horse is the first step in fully utilizing the methods of the EAGALA Model. The ES and MH alike need to work toward a full understanding of why the horse's pure, unfiltered behavior is so important and learn to fully appreciate the ways these responses can hold meaning. Working with the horse requires freeing ourselves from standard reactions and interpretations. It requires expanding our understanding of safety. It requires looking harder so we can see the information horses give us.

When we allow ourselves to work within all these many nuances, we're finally set up to fully access the power of the process. The challenge then becomes monitoring our own Apostrophe S situations, catching the SPUD'S and providing clean feedback during the session, while refraining from any particular conclusion. The client's response should always be entirely his or her own.

As a facilitator, it's not OK to rush a client into a conclusion (if we even have that opportunity). Better to allow the client to "marinate," or leave a session and figure out what to do with the situation. We don't have to direct it or be in charge of it.

This following case is called "The Grass Is Always Greener." It shows just how little control facilitators really have over what's happening with the client. It's also a clear example of the client processing between sessions and an example of just how fast clients can hit their peak in one EAGALA session and get what they need without us going any deeper. Above all else, this is a story about trusting the process.

> A mother called wanting to come out with her daughter for a session. She and her husband were living separately, with the possibility of divorce, and the fourteen-year-old daughter was really struggling with the transition. Her purpose for calling us was to help her daughter cope with the changes in their family.

> The day arrived, but Mom showed up alone. It turned out the daughter was scheduled for a school trip and couldn't be there. We checked in with Mom, who wanted to proceed with the session anyway. She wasn't very specific about her goal but said she had "a lot of stuff going on."

> I'll also mention that this was the very first session for the equine specialist, who happened to be my daughter, Sydney. Sydney had been involved in the EAGALA Model for a long time. She'd been certified several years ago, with the goal of becoming a therapist. Up to this point, she'd only done leadership and life-skill sessions with elementary-age children and youth groups. We thought this family session would be a good opportunity to get her feet wet with a more mature situation.

> To start things off, we asked the client to introduce herself to the horses. She walked around the horses for a while. Our miniature horse, Twister, stuck his head through the fence and started eating

grass. The client walked over to him and placed her hand on him. He just kind of swished his tail at her and continued eating. She stood there, petting Twister, and then nudged him to get his head up a little bit. She reached through the fence and grabbed a big bunch of grass, offering it to him with her hand. Twister didn't take it.

She did that for a few minutes, and it appeared she was getting kind of frustrated. She just kept putting grass in front of this horse, but he kept ignoring her, eating the grass where he was standing. At one point he finished eating everything in his reach and started to nibble at the dirt, continuing to ignore Mom.

The session had been going on for only eight minutes. Mom's ears and face were turning red. She was pacing in place. Sydney stepped in and said, "We noticed you are offering the horse grass. It looks like you're offering him something that he's already getting for himself."

Mom stood straight up and looked at Sydney, the color draining out of her face. Without a single word, she turned around, walked out of the arena, got in her car, and drove away.

The team was left looking at each other in an empty arena. All our Apostrophe S stuff started coming right out. "What did we do wrong? Did we apply too much pressure? Was she not ready to think about that?" Sydney felt responsible for what had happened. She knew her comment wasn't exactly a clean observation, and she was left thinking she had done something wrong. We were assuming what had happened was negative. Later on, the therapist tried to contact the mom, but the cell phone had been disconnected. We were left with no idea what was going on with this client.

Three months passed. Then the mom called and said she'd like to come back and schedule another session. She didn't say anything about what she had been doing for the past three months.

We thought it would be important to have all of the same horses in the arena, including Twister. It took some convincing, but we made sure Sydney was there again as well. When Mom showed up, she barely said hello. She had this really determined look on her face, and her shoulders were squared. "I'm ready to get started."

Upon entering the arena, the first thing she did was walk right up to Twister and put a rope around his neck. She led him out of the gate and into the round pen behind the arena; then she proceeded to shut him inside. She came back into the arena, looking totally relaxed. "Now I can get to work."

All we said was, "All right, go ahead and pick up where you left off." She introduced herself to the two remaining horses and started doing things with them. At one point she actually had them standing side by side and following her around the arena.

After a while, we checked in. "What was different between today and the last time you were here?"

She responded, "I had to take care of that little son of a bitch. It was great once I got him out of here."

We said, "What is it about that 'son of a bitch' that needed to be out of here?" It turns out she was referring to her ex-husband. She had been doing everything she could to please him, throwing herself at him to try and get him back, even though he was already in another relationship and living with someone else.

When Sydney made the comment, "Looks like you're offering him something that he can get for himself," it hit her full force. What she did with Twister was exactly what she did with her husband—and she knew exactly what she had to do.

After leaving the arena that day, she took care of things—got a new cell phone and had her old one cut off, hired a lawyer, got a full-time job (her first since getting married), sold the house, and got an apartment she could afford whether her husband provided support or not. She said she wasn't ready to come back until she put things into place. So when she came back to us, she came with a plan, ready to focus on the future with her daughter. We asked about her daughter and she said, "You know, my daughter's fine. It was really me that needed this."

What is interesting is that while Twister—a.k.a. the son of a bitch in her metaphor—was in the round pen, he was pitching a fit, kicking and screaming and hollering. But the other two horses never even looked his way and didn't feed into his energy at all. When we checked in by saying, "Now that the 'son of a bitch' is separated, he's sure making a lot of noise," her comment to us was, "I'm not even going to go there." She would look at Twister in the round pen and just shake her head. She came back a few more times and continued to make real progress in establishing her new life.

In that first session, we didn't know what the client was experiencing, and it turns out we didn't have to. We hit the session peak within ten minutes of beginning. The client got what she needed and then did all the rest. As it happens, that one horse SPUD changed her life. She made a plan and executed it without another word being spoken. It took her three months to process it, and when she came back, she was ready to face her future.

How did Sydney feel after that? Obviously it gave her some relief upon learning the real story. This case is still definitely a topic of conversation and is great learning for all of us. It reiterated that we don't truly know what's happening for a client. We can assume and guess, but sometimes the proof is in the doing rather than the saying.

So many times when we're standing there watching, we have absolutely no idea what the client might be doing, or why he or she is doing it. Although our Apostrophe S wants very badly to know what's happening, this case is a good reminder that we don't need to know.

There is a key illustration of this in the EAGALA training manual, depicting two triangles laid over the top of each other. The triangle at the forefront represents the client-horse dynamic. The triangle at the back represents the treatment team-client dynamic. Both triangles include the client.

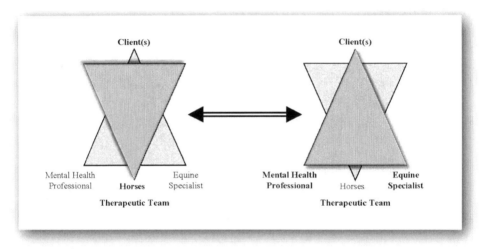

Ideally, the horse-client triangle will remain primarily in the forefront throughout the fluid, dynamic process of our sessions. Every time the treatment team steps in to interact with the client, either verbally or non-verbally, the client-horse relationship triangle slips into the background. The more the treatment team-client triangle stays in the foreground, the further away we are from equine-assisted psychotherapy and the EAGALA Model.

Of course there are times when the treatment team-client triangle is in the foreground: during check-in, during verbal processing, and during set-up of the activity. But how we influence focus through the session and learn when to shift that focus in the session is key. The triangle image can help facilitators remain mindful and keep the focus where it belongs. While the client is really engaged with the horse, we should not take that focus away.

If we're really following the model, we are making a conscious effort to get out of the client's way but are still watching and present, working to tune in to what the horses are showing us. Our solutions and our time-frame come a distant second to the horse-client triangle framework.

Facilitators need to accept that they may not know what is happening for the clients or what meaning it has for them. Such is the case in this next story.

> This next case often comes to mind when I talk about trusting the process, because once again it was a great learning moment for me about waiting to see what happens. If we are willing to just wait and be open, many things come out. I call this story "Sometimes It's Good to Just Be."

> A young man was referred to us through the Department of Juvenile Justice's Juvenile Probation Program for underage drinking and a DUI, a criminal charge for driving a vehicle under the influence of alcohol. When we got his intake material, we recognized his name right away. He was the star of our local football and swim teams. He lettered in every sport we had. Mom was a well-known attorney, and Dad was a doctor.

> Everyone knew this young man in our small town, so we had some anxiety. I looked at my MH and admitted my trepidation. "This brings up stuff for me. This is a high-profile family. What if we mess him up? We'll never work in this town again."

> When he came for his first session, we were surprised by his politeness. He emptied his pockets onto a barrel outside the arena, taking out a cell phone, a pager, a paper calendar, and a BlackBerry. We asked him how he was doing, and he just shrugged a bit. So we asked him to get to know the horses and then select one and move it around the arena. The client walked out into the arena, turned a barrel on its side, sat down, leaned up against it, and went to sleep.

> Participants in EAGALA Part One training know there is a question that asks what you would do if a client sat down on the dirt.

This client not only sat down in the dirt; he took it a step further and went to sleep! What were we going to do?

My MH and I looked at each other, surprised and wondering what to do. With our Apostrophe S in full swing, we were making all sorts of assumptions regarding respect and how it seemed this client was not taking his legal situation seriously. Maybe he thought with his affluence and fame, he could get away with anything. Beyond this, how do we justify a client sleeping during the therapy session? While our Apostrophe S was raging all over the place, one by one the horses started mingling over the client, smelling the barrels, smelling this young man. Then all four horses lay down with him.

We had two horses stretched out flat and snoring. Two others were in the dirt, propped up, heads nodding. The client was snoring; the horses were snoring. I looked over, and my partner started yawning, so I started yawning. Now we wanted to go to sleep too. And because of the horses' behavior, we started feeling curious about what was happening here.

When the session came to an end fifty minutes later, we had to walk out and wake him up. I said, "Hey, it's time to go." We gave him a second to get his bearings and then checked in. "Is there anything about the experience you'd like to share?"

All he would say is, "It was good to just be." That's it. He went and collected his things and left.

It was really hard. During the session I wanted to wake up the client so he could see what was happening. I wanted him to appreciate that horses didn't just do this; they didn't just fall asleep with you. My MH and I were also worried about the fact that he'd slept through the whole session instead of working with us. Our Apostrophe S continued placing all sorts of fears and worries about what was happening and what "should" be happening.

Next week's session came. The client went out into the arena, got his barrel, and went to sleep. There were four *new* horses in the arena, and once again, all four lay down and went to sleep.

Once again we woke him up at the end of the session. He answered the same question in the same way: "It was good to just be," and he left. Four weeks later, we now had sixteen different horses, each of which had fallen asleep with this young man. I had never seen such a unique SPUD repeat itself so consistently.

We decided that in this next session, we were going to wake him up earlier, to see if we could play off his words and get any more information. We woke him up, and this time the therapist asked a follow-up question: "I wonder where else you can 'just be,' like you are with the horses."

The young man wheeled around and said, "What?"

The therapist repeated, "We were just wondering where else you could 'just be.'"

He said, "Ma'am, you don't understand. There *is* nowhere else."

Now that he had started talking, he didn't seem to want to stop. He shared with us that he got up at five o'clock every morning. He was at the pool by five thirty, swimming. Then he went to school a half hour early every day to do student-government duties. In school he was carrying a full academic load. After school he had sports, and he played every sport. Every minute of every day was scheduled. He had zero free time.

He shared with us that he had never had a sleepover. He didn't have a normal social life because he was so driven. We asked, "Who's driving this horse for you?" and found out his mom was the one pushing him. She was from the other side of the tracks and grew up really poor but found her way out through sports. She got a sports scholarship to college and went all the way through law school. Now she was expecting him to do the same. This family could have paid for anything but instead wanted the young man to earn it on his own. She figured sports would do the same thing for him as it did for her.

The next week arrived, and when we asked him if he thought any more about where he could "just be," he shared with us that he thought maybe he would like to sleep in on Sundays. So we had him show us what that might look like, assuming he would go to sleep again. But this time he did not get the barrel and lie down. He started moving the barrels and the horses. We began to notice there was one horse who kept moving a barrel every time he set it up. The horse would grab hold of it and adjust it in some way. So we asked him about it. He said, "That's my mom." He went back to moving the barrels, and sure enough, every time he would get them in place, the "mom" horse would keep messing with it. He said, "I am working out here trying to figure it out, but every time I start, my mom interferes."

As we watched, the therapist and I were talking. "You know, a teenage boy sleeping in is probably a good way to 'just be.' I bet you he just wants to sleep until one o'clock."

My MH said, "I'll say he wants to sleep until eleven or twelve." So we asked him, "What is your plan to 'just be' and to sleep in?"

He said, "On Sunday I want to sleep in to seven thirty."

Seven thirty. Not eleven or twelve, or even one o'clock, like a normal teenager. Seven thirty. We said, "OK, why don't you try that and let us know how that works." He left.

The next day our phone lit up like a Christmas tree. Mom was irate when he got home and announced his plan. His court counselor called and said we were affecting his future by suggesting that he sleep in until seven thirty. Mom accused us of encouraging him to quit focusing on his athletics and scholarships. She wanted him pulled out of therapy.

Needless to say, we relayed what had been happening in the sessions and how little the client was asking. The court counselor, who was a pretty tough lady, admitted, "It sounds like Mom's problem, not the young man's." So he stayed in the program.

The next week he came in. We asked him, "Were you able to 'just be' over the week?"

He said, "Yeah, I got to sleep in on Sunday."

Sleeping in became the first of many steps for this client. He stayed in the program and was in treatment for quite a while, ironing out the situation. We started family sessions. Dad became very involved, but Mom never once came out. We had him do other activities with the horses to work out how he could learn to socialize with his peers, which became part of his treatment. He and his dad planned a pizza party by the pool with his friends. When he came back, we asked him how the sleepover went. He opened the gate and then proceeded to shoo the horse he called "Mom" out of the arena. His mom had actually moved out the Friday before the sleepover. When we asked him about it, he said, "It's fine...now."

Throughout the sessions, the client shared that swimming was the only thing he liked to do, but he hated to compete. What he really wanted to do was learn to play the guitar. So he started taking guitar lessons and eventually went on to college as a music major. This young man is now a music teacher, having found his own path.

Allowing time to pass as the client seemingly "slept" his way through four sessions was a real test in trusting the process. Following the path this client took meant taking an improvisational mind-set, letting go of the plan, and being willing to flex with the client to support the flow of the story…his story. By becoming congruent with the client and lying down to sleep alongside him, the horses provided the clues the team needed to know things were moving in the right direction, despite appearances. In other words, the team kept the horse-client triangle at the forefront of the sessions until the client felt his way to the heart of his situation.

Trusting the process, knowing everything that needs to happen will happen when we focus on the horses, is an advanced skill, one that can defy every aspect of our professional training. While we have goals in EAGALA sessions, such as treatment plans or identified objectives, we learn to let go of what we think the processes, solutions, and timeframes are supposed to look like.

It may be noted that change occurred for this client as soon as the team asked the key question, "I wonder where else you can 'just be'?"

So why didn't the treatment team check in with the client earlier in the process? Why did the team wait it out?

Timing is a skill each treatment team needs to develop. There is a time for the team to step in and bring the treatment team-client triangle into the forefront, but there is also a time to allow the process to unfold, when the experience and the horses need to do their work. The skill comes with knowing which is which. Too early, and the client is not emotionally ready to disclose.

Patterns need to be allowed to develop and mature, so the client can come to a place where it's safe to disclose. The first occurrence of a Unique aspect is chance, and the second occurrence starts to validate. Three or more occurrences become a Pattern, indicating a clear message—something deeply meaningful to the client is happening.

In "Sometimes It's Good to Just Be," the treatment team was right in stepping out of the way so that they didn't block the process. But in this next case, the team's Apostrophe S took over for the opposite effect.

The name of this story is "I Found My Conscience," and it's a case that really emphasizes once again how our perceptions and assumptions impacted a client experience when the client wasn't doing what we thought she needed to be doing.

We were working with a group of kids in transition, who were adjusting to divorce or struggling during some kind of change in their families or lives. In this particular session, the youths came in, and we did a check-in, where everybody shared who they were and why they were there. We gave the instructions for the session, and the group went out and started moving the horses around.

However, this one girl just went over to the gate, sat down, and stared outside the arena. Even though it was July, she had come in wearing a dark pullover hoodie with long pants. I assumed she was some kind of Goth punk kid. A couple of times, the other group members would go over and try to get the girl to join the group, but she would refuse. Because of my Apostrophe S, I labeled her for not helping her group when they asked.

The group members finally stopped trying to get this girl to join in. At the end of the session, we checked in, and they talked about what they noticed most about the horses, namely that all of the horses were different, with different sizes and colors, but that they were also basically the same too. They made a connection between the horses and their group, that while they were all different and here for different reasons, they essentially had the same problems. The group seemed to have bonded, and it was a satisfying way to wrap up the session.

We made the decision not to check in with the girl sitting by the fence; she didn't want to engage, so we just didn't engage her either. Both my MH and I had placed our labels on her. As we headed out the gate, the girl got up, and I said, "I'm sorry you didn't get anything out of today."

She looked at me funny and said, "Huh?"

Thank goodness my therapist partner caught my very unclean observation and followed up with something much cleaner. She said, "There was a 'huh' to what Mark said?"

The girl's head shot up, and she said, "Yeah, what does he know? I found my conscience today."

After she left, we debriefed about it some more. We realized we had made a lot of assumptions. It seemed like she didn't do anything, and as a result, we did not check in with her, thinking she "wasn't engaged." Yet she said, "I found my conscience." So something had happened.

The next week, the group came in. This time, the girl had a very short-sleeved shirt on, almost like a tank top, and shorts. It was now obvious that she was a "cutter," meaning she would cut on herself as a coping mechanism. The scars were very visible up and down her arms. We checked in. "How are you guys doing?"

She piped right up. "I'm doing great."

Curious, we asked, "OK, anything else you want to share about doing great?"

She said, "Nope."

So we introduced the activity, and out of the blue, this girl asked, "Hey, can we use my conscience today?"

My partner and I looked at each other and the MH said, "Well, yeah...tell us about your conscience."

She said, "You know, the little horse with the blue eye."

My miniature horse, Twister, has a blue eye. I said, "Oh, that's Conscience?" Twister was in a different paddock, just outside of the indoor arena. We hadn't even used him with this group the previous week, so I was curious how she even knew about him. But I said, "Sure, why don't we go get Conscience." So the whole group went out, got her "Conscience," and brought him into the arena.

They continued with the session. This time, she got very involved with the activities and was part of the group. We decided to end a little early to explore this "Conscience" piece a bit more with her. We checked in. "Anyone want to share about their experience?"

Everyone shared, and when we got to her, she opened right up, "Well, last week I found my Conscience, and I wanted to make sure that he was going to be here this week. Conscience stayed with me throughout the session." This was quite true; during the session, Twister had followed her everywhere. And now his name was Conscience.

She went on to share that the previous week, when she found her Conscience, she decided it was time to go tell her mom she was a cutter. She had been completely undiagnosed up to that point, hiding it from everyone, in her struggle with her parents' divorce and moving to a new town. She said she used the black hoodie and makeup to hide her scars, even though she wasn't really Goth and didn't even like heavy-metal music. She had learned, however, that hiding from people under all this makeup and clothing didn't solve anything; it caused her more problems.

"Well, how did your Conscience come for you to find it?" we asked.

She admitted she was really pissed off in the first session for having to be there. She didn't want anything to do with the group. But when she went to sit down over by the fence, she noticed a blue eye looking at her through the boards of the adjacent pen. She tried to look away, but the blue eye—Twister's—would walk over and keep putting itself in front of her field of vision. She even turned around to stare out of the back of the arena, but Twister ran down the fence and looked at her through the gaps on that side too. He was there, no matter where she tried to look.

She couldn't get away from his eye—her "Conscience." And then she made the connection that her Conscience also wouldn't let her get away from the cutting. She realized she wanted to get help.

We were blown away. While we had been making assumptions, irritated by her lack of participation, she was making a huge connection between Twister and her situation. It was one of those *wow* moments for us as a team. It was also really clear that our perceptions had impacted the client experience. By not checking in with her at the end of that first session, we forestalled her story. Thankfully the session impacted her so much that she left the farm ready to bring her situation out. When she got home, she took matters into her own hands and told her mom.

Part of trusting the EAGALA process is *trusting the client*. Facilitators tend not to trust this aspect of "trusting the process," especially when experiences with different types of clients can lead to a more cynical viewpoint. However, the trust we're referring to here is that every client—no matter what age, diagnosis, or background—has the capability to discover his or her own strengths and unique paths. In this case, the label the facilitators put on the client got in the way of trusting in her capability as a human being to discover her own answers.

Granted, there were many aspects of this client that helped the facilitators jump to conclusions. Her manner and her dress made it easy to assume certain things about her. The labeling got in the way of their ability to remain curious and remember that everything that was happening was part of the story the clients have of their lives.

Curiosity is about coming from a place of not knowing. As soon as we think we know, we slip into our agendas and place our interpretations and meaning on the experience; it becomes about the facilitators instead of about the clients and departs from trusting the process, the clients, and the horses.

One of the hardest things for most facilitators is allowing the process to unfold in ways that don't necessarily look like anything they've been trained to expect. Sometimes a lot is happening with the client, even when the team spends their time "just standing there." As one MH put it:

The horses don't get hung up on their own therapeutic brilliance. They just reflect the client in that moment, giving form and presence to what the client most needs to see or hear.[11] It took some

---

11 Margaret Kelleher, "Still Points: Letting the Horse Be the Therapist," *EAGALA in Practice* 4 no. 1 (2011): 38–39.

time to consistently trust the horses to do the work at which they are so capable, especially learning to stand quietly with my ES when, ostensibly, "nothing" was happening.

We have had many sessions in which the quietness between horses and clients was interrupted only by birds chirping outside the arena. I now realize clients who connect with the horses in this profoundly quiet way also connect with themselves differently: they tap their inner stillness, their own calm, in the face of the chaos that sometimes characterizes their lives. Instead of experiencing confirmation of a negative world view, their view is expanded in ways they never imagined possible. Clients say, "No one has ever just hung out with me like this before" and "I don't get to be this quiet at home."

Trusting the Horse

In the EAGALA Model, horses aren't simply a tool or mechanism for the therapy process; they're considered equal members of the facilitating team. The various parallels between horse/herd dynamics and human dynamics, along with the horse's ability to impact humans with their size, presence, and feedback, is vital to the progression of treatment. When human facilitators successfully harness the horse's capabilities, a process unfolds that leads clients to powerful discoveries and change.

Through the various cases presented here, we already know the many ways horses can work, even when those ways expand the limits of our own understanding. Their natural social behaviors help clients explore their own patterns, behaviors, and skills when it comes to relationships, leadership, boundaries, communication, and connection. Working in concert with horses can help clients understand and find the right balance within the complex world of human dynamics. The horse-as-facilitator equine partnership does this in a nonverbal, experiential way to optimize learning for long-term change in the client.

To achieve this ideal most successfully, the EAGALA Model recognizes horses must be allowed to access and express their most innate instincts and behavior. We *want* their deepest natural being—the horse as hyper-aware, basic prey animal. We want them to show us what we're missing. We want their response and feedback to lead the client. The horse's deep ability to sense and react naturally to its environment contributes significantly to client sessions, so we want that feedback to come from those ingrained instincts and behaviors.

It might surprise people to learn that many horses need to undergo an unlearning process, just like their human counterparts. The typical trained and modified behaviors we find in horses today are not necessarily desirable in a mental health context. It's easy to underestimate how many behaviors humans train away or disallow on a daily basis. This type of conditioning serves to dampen the horse's natural response.

However, the flip side of this means adjusting our own deeply ingrained reactions and expectations of horses and leaving ourselves completely open to possibilities we can't anticipate. What the typical horse person deems normal or acceptable may not apply in an EAGALA Model session. No matter what lens we've used in the past to work with, train, or interact with horses, standard interpretations of the horse and its behavior need to be peeled back and stripped away. This includes things we project onto our horses and the opinions we form and accept as fact about our horses. ("This horse is laid back" or "This horse is a troublemaker.") It also means adjusting our assumptions about what clients may think, learn, and believe about horses.

This includes accepting that our clients may not even *like* horses. Our relationship to the horse might be precious to us, but our love of horses is one more thing we need to put aside when the client enters the arena. What we interpret as right or wrong, good or bad, acceptable or unacceptable, no longer matters. We always have to remain open to the fact that other possibilities for interpretation might—and often do—exist in the client's mind.

Once in the arena, interpreting the horse becomes the client's job. Trusting the horse becomes our job. The client's interpretation will be perfect—for his or her situation.

Horses don't debate their actions ahead of time. They do what they need to do. This story, which I call "Dear Abby," is a case showing how horses can sometimes confront clients in a way we humans never could.

This particular client was a young man in a residential treatment facility, court ordered to be there from a history of making poor choices. "David" came out weekly with the other kids from the residential center.

One Monday morning we got a call from the residential program. "We had an incident that happened over the weekend, and the house is in chaos. We need to bring the guys out right away to sort through things. There's some accountability that needs to happen." Over the weekend, David had somehow coerced the whole staff into a food pantry, whereupon he shut the door and locked them in. That's right: he locked the staff in a food pantry, with the office door wide open and six youths loose in the cottage at the time.

David went into the office, got a credit card, called in pizza delivery, and proceeded to have a party while the staff was locked up. He then had all of the kids get ready for hygiene and go to bed. Once he was in bed himself, he asked one of the other kids to go let the staff out of the pantry. This was a very intelligent move; he knew that once he was in bed and not acting out, they couldn't lay hands on him.

How did he manipulate his peers so well? By putting them in just as much trouble as he was in. Once they followed in the peer negativity, they were caught. After the incident, the whole house was put on complete shutdown, with everyone restricted to their rooms. It was a barebones situation because they had put the staff in jeopardy, made unsafe choices, and potentially caused harm to themselves and others.

When the group got to the barn, the staff was still upset. Understandably, they felt unsafe around the kids. There needed to be some accountability to reset the balance of power.

We put three horses in the arena: a Welsh Mountain pony named Abby, a gelding named Fred, and my old gelding Mon-Jour. An activity was set up requiring the group to get all of the horses across an obstacle, an obstacle that represented this big thing that had happened. The whole group needed to be accountable for getting all the horses over the obstacle.

They played around a little bit, moving the horses around the arena. Then, all of a sudden, Mon-Jour just stopped, as if he realized they wanted him over the obstacle. So he went and jumped over the obstacle and then went over and stood against the fence as if to say, "OK, I'm done." The other horse, Fred, eventually went over the obstacle, which left Abby. This all happened within probably fifteen minutes.

So the group went after her to get her over the jump. Abby walked straight up to the obstacle until her front legs touched the pole of the jump, and then she just stood there and refused to move. The boys got frustrated, and David, the ringleader of the group, started waving his arms and hollering, trying to get the horse to move. He then went up to her and pushed her from behind with his hands. All she did was turn around and look at him.

We asked, "What is this horse thinking about what's happening here?" David responded that she didn't seem to like that.

He continued to apply pressure to her, whooping and hollering. Abby turned her head to look at him and stamped her back foot. She didn't kick out but was definitely communicating. So we checked in with David again. "What's going on now?"

He said, "Well, she's getting really irritated."

We said, "When irritation starts happening, then what?"

He responded, "Then she might get more upset if she doesn't like what we're doing." He continued working on moving Abby and then smacked this horse on the bottom of her butt. This time, she picked up both hind legs and kicked out—but not anywhere near David.

We checked in once more. "What's going on with her now?"

To this he responded, "Well, she's getting ready to knock my head off."

I turned and looked at my MH and started saying that despite this client knowing what is going on, it didn't seem to be stopping him. I knew that Abby was not going to take much more before getting really serious. Just as I started saying this to the MH, David backed up and took a run at Abby, smacking her with both hands on her backside. Abby waited until the precise moment, lifted up her back legs, and slammed them into both of *his* legs. He dropped to the ground.

We had another ES watching the session, and she went running for ice. But David picked himself right up and hollered for "circle up." In residential program-speak, they call for a circle up when there's a problem that needs to be solved or something that needs to be addressed. So David called for a circle up, and everybody came together. What was unique is all three of the horses came and joined the circle too, all facing with their heads into the circle. Abby joined in, standing right next to David.

David didn't say one word about being kicked. Instead he said, "We need to make a plan before somebody gets hurt out here."

One of the other kids then said, "No, we have to make a plan about what we're going to do about the house." They then started talking about what they were going to do to make the house safe again. Abby wasn't mentioned at all.

The residential program had already contacted David's probation officer, and a court date was set. They intended to document a probation violation, so he would be removed from the residential setting and put into juvenile detention, which was a higher level of containment. When the court date arrived, his therapist asked me to be present, so I was there along with David and the residential staff.

The judge asked David, "Is there any reason I shouldn't lock you up right now?"

David said, "Yeah, I've got a new therapist I'm working with, and I think it's going to really help."

I looked over at the residential director and said, "New therapist? Did you hire somebody?"

Meanwhile, the judge asked, "Well, is the therapist here? Is there somebody that can speak about this for you? What is this therapist's name?"

David said, "Her name is Abby."

I about fell out of my chair. I wondered how I was going to explain who Abby was. The judge asked if Abby was in the courtroom and would be willing to speak.

I raised my hand and stood up. "I'm not Abby, but I guess I'll represent her."

The judge said, "So tell me about the situation they're in now."

I told him Abby was a horse, a therapist with four legs and a tail. The judge looked skeptical. David proceeded to acknowledge that yes, Abby was a horse. But then he went on to explain she was the first therapist to hold him accountable in a way that really mattered to him. The judge was quiet for a moment and then looked hard at

David and gave him six more weeks at the residential center, after which time we were going to come back with a progress report.

Well, Abby's confrontation was a turning point for David. From that moment forward, he shifted in leaps and bounds, making enough progress to transition into a therapeutic foster home. Within those six weeks, it was evident that he was making big strides. Abby's literal kick in the pants that day had done the job.

David was a savvy young man. He knew his client rights and knew how to play the game. At one point in his care, he'd demanded the residential staff take him to the hospital for a simple paper cut, so there's no doubt he could have used Abby's literal kick in the pants to evoke his client rights and quit treatment. Instead, after he got kicked, he didn't even share that he got hurt. We had to ask him to show us where she'd kicked him, to fill out the incident report. His caseworker had to pry information out of him to get any acknowledgment about the kick, and so did his probation officer. So instead of using it to his advantage, David went from extreme attention seeking to being accountable—all based on this single interaction with Abby.

For us, it was really about trusting the process and absolutely trusting the horse. This client was headed down a bad path, a path that probably would have been worse than anything Abby could have done to him.

This case reinforces a couple of key principles in the EAGALA Model. The most important again is that we should not apply standard interpretations to the horse's actions in a session; that is the *client's* job. In this case, while the facilitators saw a horse reacting in a manner that would typically be defined as inappropriate, the client saw the horse's actions from a completely different perspective. Someone was finally holding him answerable for his actions. Someone finally helped him clearly understand the implications of those actions.

In other equine-based mental health models, the horse isn't necessarily allowed this kind of freedom, the freedom to bring the session to a peak, as Abby did in this case. In the EAGALA Model, horses walk freely and are given the space to be themselves. Facilitators are trained to develop the feel and timing that allow the session to reach its peak through the horse, with minimal interference. Teams are taught to improvise when horses and clients take things in another direction. Granting horses the autonomy to *act* requires human facilitators to develop flexibility and a profound trust in the horse.

It also requires facilitators to become much more observant in the present moment. Despite being such a large animal, the horse is capable of being extremely subtle and refined in its nonverbal communication. Once we respect and acknowledge that subtlety, the horse SPUD'S tend to become more and more evident. It's usually our awareness of equine psychology and body language that needs to become more attuned.

Granted, as facilitators we do not want clients to get kicked or hurt. We are not oblivious to safety, nor do we simply allow unsafe things to happen as a normal course of action. Each time the treatment team stepped in to ask David what was going on, it was a safety intervention. Interestingly, despite his apparent awareness of the warning messages Abby was giving him, he didn't change his behavior. In this situation, we had a client who demonstrated an inability to react appropriately to the verbal and nonverbal signals in his daily environment, a situation that repeated itself in the arena. The arena mirrored exactly what was going on in his residential treatment and other areas of his life. Because of this, the team chose to explore the dynamic to see where it would go. In the end, Abby was the only one who finally confronted him in a way that he could hear and understand.

Here's a case from Mark's early awareness building, where the horse once again (literally) held a client responsible, even while outside a formal session, a case that continues to challenge our perception of horses' capabilities.

The name of this story is "He Knows Me." When I first started EAGALA work, I was working in a residential setting for sexually aggressive and abusive youths. We had two components—EAGALA Model therapy and a horsemanship program.

There was a new client who hadn't progressed far enough in the program to come to the barn yet, so I hadn't met him. But when we took a group of the youths to a local horse show, the staff included him in a group who came along to watch. I was introduced to "Jimmy" at the end gate. We introduced him to the horses, a pony named Sarah and my horse, Mon-Jour.

Jimmy was standing on Mon-Jour's right side, petting him. Mon-Jour's ears were forward, and he seemed relaxed. However, after a few minutes Jimmy moved over to Mon-Jour's left side, and Mon-Jour immediately laid his ears back and leaned in like he was going to try to bite him. Jimmy moved back to Mon-Jour's right side, and the horse relaxed again.

A little while later, Jimmy moved over to Mon-Jour's left side again, and Mon-Jour reacted by pulling away from the client who was holding him. He laid his ears back, popped his lips, and acted like he was going to bite Jimmy. Jimmy moved back to the right side, and Mon-Jour was fine.

Then Jimmy moved over to Mon-Jour's left side a third time. Mon-Jour pulled completely away from the client who was holding him, stepped over to Jimmy, and knocked him to the ground. He proceeded to hold Jimmy down on the ground, mouth open on him but not actually biting.

I was still in my early days doing EAGALA Model work. At that moment, I was in "horsemanship mode," not in "EAGALA co-therapist mode" at all, so I failed to process the situation from an EAGALA mind-set. I just moved quickly to pull Mon-Jour off Jimmy and get the young man back on his feet. "I'm sorry that he did this. I don't know what's going on." I'd never seen my horse act like this. Never. So I loaded him straight into the horse trailer. Once inside, Mon-Jour beat and thrashed and stomped in that trailer, still clearly agitated. I couldn't understand what was going on and seriously wondered if Mon-Jour had developed a brain tumor or something. We ended the show and returned to the facility.

Jimmy was scheduled to come to the barn for EAGALA the next week, but he didn't complete the required "safety plan," an exercise clients do prior to any given situation where they might be required to take care of themselves. The safety plan ensured kids would know what tools to use in the event they didn't feel safe in the arena.

Another week went by, and Jimmy was once again scheduled to come to the barn. Once again, he didn't do his safety plan. So the MH and I decided we would take Mon-Jour and just go up to the day-treatment center anyway. We thought perhaps Jimmy was afraid of the horses after his incident at the horse show and that maybe bringing a horse to *him* might help him to address it.

We pulled up to the building. Jimmy came out and said, "I hope you know I'm not working with Mon-Jour today."

I said, "You know, it's understandable for you to be afraid of Mon-Jour after your experience."

Jimmy said, "Afraid? Who said I was afraid?"

I said, "Well, you haven't done your safety plan for coming to the barn."

He said, "That's not because I'm afraid."

The therapist said, "If you're not afraid of him, why don't you want to work with him?"

He looked at us and said, *"Because he knows me."*

The therapist and I looked at each other, then I asked Jimmy, "What are you talking about?"

"He knows what I was going to do."

At that point the client opened up and disclosed to us that his sexual offenses occurred at school. He would volunteer to take special-needs children to the bathroom, where he would then proceed to sexually offend on them.

At the horse show, there was a young boy in a wheelchair who was meeting Sarah, the pony. Jimmy managed to walk by this child three times. On the third time, he was able to touch the back of the young boy's head and wheelchair with his hand. Jimmy was triggered and about to make an attempt to act out. His intention was to separate from the staff and get near the boy in the wheelchair.

This boy in the wheelchair was on Mon-Jour's left side. When Jimmy stood on Mon-Jour's right side, the horse was between him and the young boy. But every time Jimmy moved to Mon-Jour's left side in an effort to get near the wheelchair, Mon-Jour would move into action. When Jimmy made his third attempt to get near the child, that's when Mon-Jour pulled away and pinned him to the ground.

Mon-Jour broke Jimmy's offending cycle by stopping him. In Jimmy's mind, he didn't think the horse was trying to hurt him; he thought the horse was trying to keep the boy in the wheelchair safe from him.

Now that the truth was out and we realized what was behind Mon-Jour's actions, we could act on it. We set up Jimmy's treatment plan so that he would work with Mon-Jour on a daily basis. And as he worked through his treatment, he would sometimes use the phrase, "I can't work with Mon-Jour today," as a safe way to share that he was in his offending cycle emotionally and did not feel safe being in the community. He created his own treatment plan, where Mon-Jour would hold him accountable. Once again, we learned to trust the horse in his actions. We couldn't have done what Mon-Jour did.

Mon-Jour became a horse I trusted more than I trust most people, and we were fortunate enough to have him for this work. Before he died at age thirty-two, I saw him intervene physically with clients. But the thing about it is every time he'd intervene physically, he never hurt anybody. He was able to do what we couldn't do. When an incongruent client was in his presence, he had a way of letting us know.

For both equine specialists and mental health professionals, stepping into equine-assisted work through the EAGALA Model can be a humbling experience no matter what. It takes a conscious effort, an ongoing self-awareness, to maintain curiosity, openness, and fluidity. The partnership of the facilitating team once again becomes a key element when both partners work to keep each other focused and open. Trusting the process is about acknowledging our "Apostrophe S" in its various forms, trusting the client, and trusting the horse. Above all else, it's maintaining a "yes, and" willingness to explore other aspects of the situation: "Yes, I realize I'm making an assumption here...and maybe there's something I don't understand. Let's explore it further."

More often than not, when we trust the process of the EAGALA Model, the client's right path *will* manifest, often in unexpected ways, but exactly as it needs.

CHAPTER 7

The Concept of Safety— Physical and Emotional

Physical and emotional safety are concerns in every therapeutic model, but it's not unusual for physical safety to become a big focus in equine-based models, especially for those new to or inexperienced around horses. Typical questions include: How safe are horses? What constitutes safe and unsafe behavior? How do we manage safety aspects?

This lends itself to one of the powerful benefits of this work with horses. Safety is a big part of life. Our drive for self-preservation—with emotional safety many times taking precedence over physical safety—impacts decisions and behaviors that have both healthy and unhealthy results. Working with horses naturally brings up these metaphors of risk and safety and the roles they play in our lives. In reality, the answers to the typical questions indicated above are once again held by the clients and relate to their lives. It is common for the safety aspects of horses to provide some of the most powerful moments in doing EAGALA Model sessions.

While safety is a great metaphoric opportunity for clients, it also presents challenges for the facilitating team. As professionals, we also come with our beliefs, backgrounds, traumas, and overall filtered lens in how we view and approach safety—physical and emotional. We need to balance this background with knowing when to step in and when to allow the horses and clients to continue playing the story out for the benefit of the client experience. This is an area that reinforces the focus on the Apostrophe S and how important this self-awareness and the team approach is in the outcomes of sessions.

Horses and Safety

Horses can often intervene with clients in ways we never could. There are multiple cases of clients finally coming to an understanding of their behavior only because of the horses' clear and definite feedback. Clients can learn from the horse's response—including the consequences of ignoring them. Because their interaction is taking place in a real-time, experiential setting, the client can further experiment with and adjust his or her behavior until achieving the desired response from the horse.

This knowledge can then provide the connection between behavior and outcomes that previously eluded the clients' understanding. With horses, clients can also explore the balance of assertiveness and collaboration required to achieve the skills needed for successful interactions in the human world.

Make no mistake—horses are also large and gregarious animals whose movement and reactions have the potential to hurt people. How do we trust our horses to do the right thing? When a horse is moving in very active or dynamic ways, how can we know that the client's learning will outweigh the risks and the session will remain physically and emotionally safe?

One aspect of this is the importance of communication between EAGALA practitioners and the agencies, funders, and individuals who are referring to EAGALA programs. When the parallel between the client's life situations and what is happening in the arena is so apparent, it becomes easier to understand the value of the model and how the horses are playing out exactly what is happening in the client's life, providing opportunities for clients to work through in no other setting. Practitioners need to work constantly to educate and clarify the differences between real and perceived safety issues and to help other professionals understand how the subject of safety can also present many rich areas of opportunity and discovery for clients.

I'd been doing EAGALA Model work for three years before I had my first incident report at the residential treatment facility. The incident involved a client tripping in front of a horse and the horse accidentally stepping on him. He didn't really get hurt but was shaken up and a bit bruised.

I did my incident report and faxed it to all the pertinent people. Within fifteen minutes my phone was ringing with staff members expressing strong concerns. Some wanted to call an emergency meeting. Others wanted to consult a vet, while others wanted to euthanize the horse or place him in another facility.

I was surprised by the reaction, especially because, knowing the horse and the situation, it was not at all like how it was being perceived.

So to get some perspective, I went to the files and checked on other incident reports from the facility. There was a folder for incident reports at the barn, which was empty. There were also folders for incident reports pertaining to the residential and educational programs at the facility. I was surprised to find the residential folder had a stack of incident reports that was *inches* thick. I pulled them out and started looking through everything from the last six months. I found reports on all kinds of incidents, including multiple injuries on the basketball court (involving broken ankles with pins and surgery) and injuries from a sledding incident where clients were cinched up in a trash bag and sent down a hill before colliding with a barbed-wire fence (resulting in two hundred stitches).

I took this evidence to the meeting and starting showing everyone the comparison between the EAGALA program and the rest of the facility. Needless to say, I made my case.

When we add horses to the mix, we need to anticipate a different response from non–horse people. We need to understand how easily misconceptions can arise. We have to be ready and provide the understanding and perspective they need to see differently.

Within the EAGALA Model, there are many, many stories of horses responding to clients in extraordinary ways, ways that seem to acknowledge and protect that client in moments of fragile emotional vulnerability. It's easy to marvel at these examples of the equine-human relationship, examples that seem to point to the horse's innately gentle nature and clearly win people over.

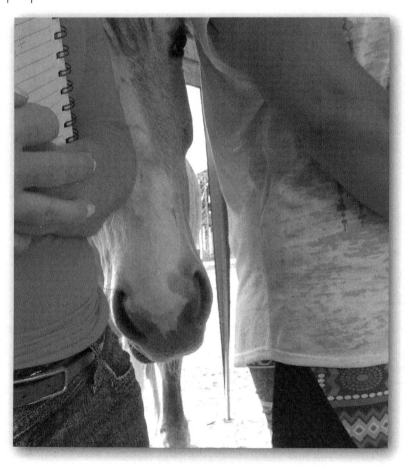

However, horses always have the capacity to surprise us, showing us unseen pathways we could never expect. This chapter contains specific case stories in which the team's concept of safety was challenged in very unusual ways. These cases are utilized here not because they are typical but because they illustrate specific points and highlight some of the complexity around the topic of safety. In every case, the client's emotional safety trumped everything else.

In the following case, the client finds her own ingenious solution for her emotional safety, one that profoundly impacts her parents and shifts them into the change they needed.

We had a family come in to iron out their parenting-style differences. The family had a young daughter, who came with them to the session. To get a better idea of what was going on, we asked them to go out and build a structure that represented their family. Everybody had to agree on what this symbol would look like.

All three family members walked out together, hand in hand. The horses turned their heads and bodies and ears toward them. But as the family got closer, all of the horses laid their ears back, turned around, and walked away. My partner and I checked in with each other. "Well, that's pretty interesting." The family looked totally unified—hand in hand, side by side, shoulder to shoulder— but the horses told us something different.

Soon the daughter pulled away and walked off on her own. Mom and Dad kept trying to approach the horses, who again moved away with their ears back. Dad moved around the horses and found a pile of PVC pipes, which he used to start constructing the structure to symbolize their family. Mom saw what he was doing and said, "Hey, hold on a minute. We aren't doing it together,"

Dad replied, "Well, this is the way I envision it."

Soon they were into it, standing face to face and disagreeing with each other. As they were arguing, one of the horses walked over and used his nose to knock down the structure Dad was building. Dad got upset. Even though Mom wasn't part of building it, she went over and started setting it back up the way he'd had it. This began a cycle where Mom and Dad would be in the middle of setting up the pieces, and a horse would knock it over. This went on repeating itself for a while, with the parents all caught up in building and rebuilding.

The more the horses knocked it over, the louder and more animated Mom and Dad became. While this was happening, we also observed the daughter. It appeared as if she had "lost herself in the crowd," as she was standing almost out of sight behind the horses. After some time, the daughter knelt down, got flat on her stomach, and crawled underneath the horse's belly so she could look out between his front legs.

My Apostrophe S kicked right into high gear, feeling this wasn't safe. But I was smart enough to hold back, keeping my eyes peeled for the slightest movement from Mr. Cool, the horse she was hiding under. Just to be sure, I moved a little closer to him, so I had his eye and his ear. I noticed that every once in a while, the girl would reach out and touch Mr. Cool's leg, as if to let him know she was still there. Then my miniature donkey, Jack, walked over and lay down right in front of Mr. Cool. Now the daughter was looking between the legs of Mr. Cool, with the donkey lying immediately in front of them. Oddly enough, this made me feel a little bit better. Mr. Cool couldn't really move unless he figured out how to step around the donkey.

Meanwhile, Dad and Mom were engaged with the rest of the horses in a throwdown with their obstacles. They'd build something, and the horses would knock it down. It was almost like a game, but the parents were getting really upset.

We arrived at the end of the session. "Hey, folks, let's wrap it up. Come on over, and we'll talk about this." The parents came over and only then realized the daughter was missing. We simply watched as they both started looking around. Mom was the first to spot her underneath the legs of a large horse. She gasped, "What are you doing down there?"

The daughter called out, "He's giving me shelter."

Mom stopped in her tracks. "What are you talking about?"

The daughter responded, "Well, he's taking care of me, and you all aren't. You're just fighting." Mom and Dad just stood there without a whole lot to say.

We said, "What do you guys think about this horse standing over your daughter? She says that he's taking care of her and you aren't."

That question had a lot of impact for the parents. They both knew that being under the feet of a horse was inherently unsafe, yet their daughter sought it out anyway because it was safer than being in their midst while they were trying to prove each other wrong. They saw how they were losing her in the middle of their fighting. It was a true moment of clarity in that first session.

We continued with this family for several sessions, and they did improve their communication. Through additional work, the daughter was able to explain that she acted out at school in order to spend time in the guidance counselor's office, where she felt like she was heard. The guidance counselor's office was the only place where she felt connection.

This was one case where we could always tell how any given session with the family was going to go. If the horses were standoffish and laid their ears back, there was some stuff to work out that day. But if the horses approached them with their ears forward, the family had done what they needed to do, and they were on the right track. The horses were a great barometer for this family, but that first session continued to be the touch point that really impacted them.

For me, the safety piece of "She is sitting under a horse" gave me a lot to think about. In all honesty, I can admit my Apostrophe S centered on what *other* people would think because I allowed that to even happen, but I look at the big picture and see things differently. The girl was taking care of her emotional safety by "taking shelter" under Mr. Cool. She actually had contact with the horse, and he knew she was there. Secondly, the donkey was lying right in front of the horse, almost acting as a barrier. In order for the horse to move, the donkey would first have to move. I know that somehow the two of them knew what was at stake and literally took care of the client.

Here's another case illustrating the concept of a client's emotional versus physical safety, while at the same time breaking a typical safety rule in the horse world. Allowing our normal horse rules to take precedence in this instance would have represented a tremendous failure to respect the client's emotional needs and created yet another barrier to his change. A key skill set for facilitators is observing the horse's body language to tell us what is needed.

I call this next case "He Can See My Soul." One of our clients from the youth residential program came out for an individual session. Back in these earlier days, the clients were learning some specific horsemanship skills, and in this case the client had learned typical safety lessons around horses, with one lesson being not to stand behind a horse. Yet here in this first session, he was working with our old horse, Fred, and we noticed that he kept standing at the rear end of the horse, sometimes leaning up against Fred, sometimes standing just a bit behind—but always he stayed well within the kick zone.

I was watching Fred, and his body language gave me no indication he was inclined to kick. But of course, my Apostrophe S went into high gear anyway. I chatted with my MH partner, wondering what this client was doing and if he was pushing boundaries or trying to get a reaction from us out of it. After discussing it and watching Fred's responses, we decided to let it play out and see where this story was going. We realized we were making a lot of assumptions about the client and his reasons when Fred was telling us it was all OK.

The first session ended, and then through the next two sessions, the client continued to place himself at the rear end of the horse. Once this dynamic became a pattern over the sessions, we decided it was time to check in about it, asking him, "The horse has had you behind him this whole time. In fact, I don't think we have seen the horse with you in front of him at all."

He looked at me and said, "Mr. Mark, I *know* darn well what will happen back here, and I'm prepared to face it. I know that he can kick me, and I know that he can hurt me. But up there, I don't know what's going to happen."

That took us by surprise. We asked, "What do you mean you don't know what's going to happen? What do you think is going to happen?"

He replied, "Well, he can see my soul, and I don't know what will happen if he sees my soul."

Wow. We had been so focused on that physical-safety piece, and yes, the client was completely aware of the possible safety issues of standing behind the horse. What he wasn't prepared to do was stand where the horse could see him head on, where he could "see" his soul. That situation was even scarier—it was about his emotional safety.

Our projection and our original story why he was doing this couldn't have been more opposite of the client's. So we asked the client what he wanted to do. He said, "Well, I really like Fred, and I really want to work on our relationship, but I'm not ready for him to see my soul." Our treatment plan evolved so he would work himself along to the point where he was willing to share his soul with Fred.

This process took several months. Sometimes he made forward progress, and sometimes he went backward. It was a really interesting journey, and that one powerful metaphor became our guiding force in his treatment plan. The day that he was able to stand in front of Fred and be "seen," without any negative consequences as a result, was a huge day.

This case is only one example of why we are very deliberate in how we address safety. Everything clients and horses do has potential meaning and parallels to life. While we can choose to teach our beliefs around what is safe or unsafe, we may be thwarting potential metaphors and opportunities because we've told them in advance how to interpret these things. We actually close down a host of possible avenues to discovery. Instead we stand back and observe, letting the clients show us where their perceptions of safety—or lack thereof—can inform our understanding of their boundaries, self-preservation, and awareness.

This is the case of another client who really challenged my beliefs about safety in the EAGALA Model. Before he was done, this client triggered almost every Apostrophe S that I had as an equine professional. I focused on my story and interpretation of this young man, versus being curious, and later learned the difference. The title of this story is "Socks and Shoes."

140

This client was part of a boys' group who were in therapeutic foster care, some in group homes and some as individuals referred by the local mental health agency. As they entered the arena on the first day, this young man, "Ethan," got my attention right off the bat. He was wearing headphones and a portable CD player. Seeing this, I had a negative reaction because we had told the agency and the clients that there was to be no electronics. I checked in with my MH team member about it, and despite it being against the rules, we decided to let it play out. Yet even with that, I had a hard time not feeling that this young man was testing boundaries and could be a troublemaker.

He stood off from the other guys as we circled up. We gave them the instructions for this session and stepped away. As soon as we moved away from the group, Ethan moved right next to me. Every time I moved, he moved. I couldn't do anything without him being stuck right next to me.

Now he was really pushing my boundaries. I'd just finished working five years with adolescent sexual offenders, and my Apostrophe S fired off again. *What is up with this client? Is he a sexual offender or what?* My MH assured me he wasn't, but he was practically stuck on me like glue.

So we decided to slip out and stand on the outside of the gate, which involved physically opening up the gate just a few inches, squeezing through, and then immediately closing it to keep him in. He stood there for a moment after we shut the gate. Then he went over to a corner of the arena, grabbed a metal chair, and flung it as hard as he could toward the horses. He next picked up another chair and flung it as hard as he could at the other kids. He picked up a third chair and swung it at the gate, hitting the metal where my partner and I were standing.

What was interesting is that neither the horses nor the boys moved when he threw the chairs in their direction. In fact, out of the three parties, guess who jumped and moved the most? The treatment team.

At this point, I was fed up and wondering what to do. I turned to my MH to discuss what kind of intervention we ought to do, but then Ethan did an about face. As soon as he finished throwing the chairs, he walked to a barrel, sat down, and took his socks and shoes off. *Now what?* we were wondering. We watched as he approached each horse, completely barefooted. He lifted his foot up for the horses to smell, touched their legs with his foot, and finally drew circles around their hooves with his own feet.

As soon as he finished showing his feet to all of the horses, he changed direction yet again. He joined the group, went along, and did everything his peers were doing. At the end, when we circled up and checked in about their experience, nobody mentioned a thing about the shoes coming off. Nobody mentioned a thing about the CD player or his headphones. Nobody mentioned anything about the chairs being thrown. I looked at my MH, and she gave the cue to just stay quiet about it as well. Needless to say, after this session was over, I needed quite the debriefing session with my MH partner to process what had happened and all the things it was triggering in me, especially around safety and the assumptions I was making about this client.

The next week, the group came in. We circled up, gave them the instructions, and started the activity. Ethan still had his CD player and headphones on, but he didn't take his shoes off or throw things. He joined the group and went along with everything.

At the end, we checked in, and everybody started talking about their experience. We just happened to throw the question out there, "What was different with the horses today versus last week?"

When it got to Ethan, he said, "Well, I didn't have to take my shoes off."

My ears pricked up. One of the other boys said, "Yeah, what was that about? You know the horses poop out here. Why didn't you take your shoes off this time?"

He said, "Well, I felt safe today."

In my mind, the story I had told myself was that this client was acting out, being very unsafe on purpose, and seeing how far he could push the limits. Now he'd completely shifted my thinking.

In EAGALA training we're taught to stop and look at opposites. So we asked him, "What are some times when you feel unsafe?"

He shared with us that he lived in a domestic-violence situation at home. There were times when things got so bad, he had to sneak out of the house to get help or to just leave. To do this, he would take his shoes off because it was quieter and allowed him to run faster.

When he met the horses on that first day, he didn't know if he'd have to run away to keep himself safe. So the first thing he did was throw the chairs, just to see how everyone would react when he was acting his worst. Then he took his shoes off until he knew he was OK. All of this was a very ingenious, deliberate, and systematic approach to ascertain when things felt safe enough to join the group. So another piece of the puzzle fell into place.

The one piece that remained was the story behind his CD player and headphones. My therapist partner and I had talked and made a decision. "None of the other kids have mentioned it. The horses haven't brought it to our attention. Let's just sit on it and see what happens."

About three sessions later, we were circled up, getting ready to start the session. Twister, the miniature horse, came over, walked right through the middle of us, and split up the group. On his way through, he reached over with his mouth, grabbed the CD player, and took off. Ethan dropped to his knees and became hysterical. Two of the other boys ran off to chase Twister and get the CD player back.

We approached Ethan to check in and calm him down. In the middle of this, I heard one of the group members behind me say, "Mr. Mark, Mr. Mark." I turned, and he said, "Mr. Mark, look."

He turned the CD player over, and I saw there was no back to it, no guts. It wasn't even a working CD player. We finished calming Ethan down and asked him to explain. Ethan shared that he was now living in therapeutic foster care after Mom had killed Dad during a fight. This CD player was the last thing he had from his home. "It was a good Christmas. My dad got me that CD player, and it's the last thing I have that's mine. You know, Mr. Mark, even the underwear I have on right now has somebody else's name in it."

All of the stuff I had been telling myself about this client was completely wrong. The CD player, even broken, was a precious commodity to him. It was an emotionally safe object for him to have. In fact, *everything* Ethan did was done to protect his emotional and physical safety.

The next week the therapist called me to let us know the other boys had collected enough money to buy Ethan a new CD player and headphones. She asked if we thought it was OK to give it to him during our session. I said, "Sure, bring it in. But be prepared—tell the boys that he may not accept it."

Sure enough, he didn't accept it when the group tried to give it to him. So we said we'd keep it, just in case he decided to change his mind. Two weeks later he asked for it. What was interesting is he felt comfortable enough with the group that he never wore headphones or the player again during sessions.

Walking through the arena barefoot; lying underneath a horse's belly; intentionally standing behind a horse—these are just a few ways the emotional safety of clients has manifested in the arena, ways that can really challenge and expand our understanding of safe versus unsafe and how clients discover their own solutions. If facilitators impede this process, stepping in at the wrong time, how much is the emotional safety of the client compromised or potentially harmed?

That being said, there are also times when facilitators do need to step in, when the threshold of safety is pushed too far. At any time, we can call a client in to explore the behaviors and reactions of the horses. Discussing this, we can gain insight into their own behaviors while also removing them from an unsafe situation. There is a balance to keep between knowing when to step in and when to allow a process to play out.

The following story is a case in which the team worked to maintain that balance in order for the horse to impact the client's change in behavior.

I call this case "Extreme Activities," and it's the case of a fifteen-year-old client who was basically a good young man but hooked into risky behavior for the adrenaline rush it provided. If his dad would ask him to trim tree limbs, he would climb the tree and start cutting off the limb he was sitting on. He raced motorcycles and, at one point, mixed jet fuel into the gasoline and blew up the bike. He caught the house on fire.

In short, he was an adrenaline junkie with a distinct knack for getting into danger before he realized what was happening.

He kept finding himself in situations his parents considered unsafe and was finally referred to us by his mom, who had literally locked up all the knives in the house and taken away all the candles—anything she could think of that could harm him and their house. His parents realized these things weren't just accidents; they were the result of something more significant.

We had several sessions with him. In the beginning he was fairly compliant, working on a basic relationship with the horses. Then we started adding different components, and sure enough, little things started happening. In each instance he was brought into new awareness, but only after the fact.

For example, he was leading a horse and decided to jump across the creek behind the barn. He jumped, but the horse pulled back. The client not only fell into the creek but got a rope burn.

When we processed the incident, he said he was "bored" on this side of the creek and wanted to play with the horse on the other side of the creek. He said it didn't even cross his mind that the horse wouldn't follow him, so when the horse pulled back and said no, he held on, and the rope burned his hand. He was aware of the bad decision; he knew he'd "done it again."

This case was a real struggle for us in every single session. This young man kept us on our toes, trying to balance his emotional safety with physical safety while also making sure he didn't do something to actually get hurt. In nearly every single session, there was a "what now" moment when maintaining that line was very trying, and the intersection of our Apostrophe S's and real risk were getting mighty close together. On one hand, we needed to allow this client the opportunity to get himself into trouble and respond to his actions. On the other, he kept putting himself in situations that caused us to watch, moment by moment, for danger. We had to keep our eye on the big picture rather than react to every little thing. It became easy to understand how his parents felt.

Things finally came to a head one week when we asked him to take the horse and assemble props in the arena to resemble his risk taking. We wanted him to label the risks he took. He went about assembling and labeling props. Then he decided to put a halter and lead rope on the horse to keep the horse alongside him. He was in the midst of trying to pick up and carry the props. He had his hands full, so he draped some of them on the horse's back so he could carry all his "risky" things with him.

He was having trouble coordinating it all. Finally, in order to keep ahold of the horse, he literally took the lead rope and wrapped it *around his own neck*. My heart jumped, and we responded, "Hey, Jeff!"

He turned to look at us, and when he did that, the rope tightened a little bit. He froze in place. "Oh, shit!" Then he very, very carefully unwrapped the rope from around his neck, his eyes wide and his face white.

We ignored our own pounding hearts and checked in. "What happened, Jeff?"

He said, "I almost did it again."

"You almost did what?"

He replied, "I almost did something stupid before I thought about it. If my horse had pulled on me like he did when I tried to get him across the creek, he could have broken my neck."

"So what was that about, when you put the rope around your neck?"

He said his hands were full, but he not only wanted to keep the horse with him but also keep all of the "risky" and "exciting" props/behaviors with him as well.

This incident marked the very first time he had ever caught himself before it was too late.

What was interesting about working with this client is the horses in each session always showed signs, like us, of being on full alert. Their heads were always up, their ears forward, eyes and nostrils enlarged. He always seemed to migrate toward one horse in particular, a very laid-back mare. But in his sessions, she was always in flight mode, moving very quickly, with sharp movements. It wasn't her typical reaction to clients.

In the aftermath of this particular session, the horses in the arena were now noticeably changed when they were around Jeff. After that day, the horses were visibly more relaxed, not on guard to such a high degree. This shift in the horses may be what really told us the client had finally turned a corner.

Since this time, Jeff was able to find ways that appropriately directed his adrenaline needs. He now has a career in extreme sports and is a television commentator for a national sports network.

While always being observant and aware, we also need to be aware that other layers of motivation might be lurking behind the overt behaviors we're seeing. When observed closely, the horses often provide the real truth behind any given client action, alerting us to the presence of a deeper story behind the behavior.

As was the case in "Socks and Shoes," the horses might exhibit calmness in the face of chaotic client behavior. Or, as in "Extreme Activities," they might exhibit agitation or flight behavior when we think a client is acting calmly. Each stands in full contrast to our immediate perceptions. Knowing, trusting, and reading our horses' behaviors and the messages they are giving us, trusting the process, and ongoing training and self-awareness of the facilitators are keys in managing the complexity of both physical and emotional safety and the therapeutic needs of our clients. Of particular importance is recognizing the power emotional-safety needs have even over physical safety.

Safety and risk are primary issues in many clients' lives and a sensitive topic for practitioners of the EAGALA Model. It takes skill on the part of the team to facilitate the session while monitoring and making effective decisions around the safety variables. When facilitators can hold this space successfully, safety is a powerful dynamic for moving the client forward.

CHAPTER 8

Structuring Sessions and the Art of Improv

Choosing What We Do in Sessions

This book is full of actual case examples resulting from client sessions. As facilitators, how do we choose what to set up for the client session in the first place? What activities do we utilize?

Session structure is key to initiating the power of the client experience. Practitioners soon learn the EAGALA Model is not about setting up an activity for the sake of an activity. There is an entire thought process and purpose behind everything we do. While session structure as a topic is much more extensive than the scope of this book, there are some key principles we take into account.

Metaphor

As mentioned earlier, everything in the arena is a parallel to life. Part of the power of the EAGALA Model is that clients are able to create in the outside realm a symbolic, physical representation of what is happening in their internal selves. Everything in the arena space has the potential to become a metaphor, whether it is the horses, the gate, a bird, the dirt, or a barrel.

When starting with a client, facilitators structure opportunities based on the treatment or learning goals. They set up the space and horses to allow the client to begin assembling his or her symbolic story. Typical activities tend to fall in four different categories:

- Observation: Watching the horses, clients begin to project meaning onto what they see, which in turn shares aspects of themselves and their belief systems in an emotionally safe way. Spending time observing provides an opportunity to view aspects of their life from a distanced, outside perspective.
- Relationship: Having clients spend time developing relationships with the horses begins revealing the dynamics they employ and the types of relationships they have with others, things, or themselves.
- Movement/no movement: Movement has broad and powerful applications metaphorically and can be about change and transition. Moving toward a prop, an object, or a person in the session can correspond with moving toward a goal or person in life. Moving away from something can represent moving away from fear or an unhealthy place. Working with the horses to move or have them not move brings up many of these metaphorical moments.
- Creating: Spending time in the space, building or creating physical representations, whether with items or horses, has an impact by once again placing into the physical realm dynamics within the client that can otherwise be abstract or hard for them to articulate, define, or understand.

Through the process of these many types of session experiences, the client's story begins to unfold. In this next story, take note of how observation, relationship, movement, and creating all played a part in the client's unfolding story.

This story is called "Bird's-Eye View." "Jane" was an outpatient client referred to us from another organization. She was also a licensed therapist who wasn't currently practicing. Initially she shared that she had relationship issues, and so we started there, inviting her to begin developing relationships with the horses.

151

During this process, she would single out one horse and move toward it in such a way that the horse would immediately move away from her. Several times the horse would move away and then stop and really look at her, almost like a standoff. She kept telling us this was how men treated her.

As we started gathering more information, we found out she wasn't practicing as a therapist because her license had been suspended. She had several restraining orders against her from different men. She participated in some sort of dance group, and at the group functions, she would find a dance partner and then become completely obsessed with that person, calling him and following him. She recognized that her approaches to relationships were not working.

In sessions, my horse, Fred, kept moving away from her but would then also move toward her in ways that would make her move quickly in response. Sometimes, if she approached him really quickly, he would stop, look at her, and then move toward her swiftly, with his ears laid back. She saw this as him "confronting" her. There were many times she would have insights that seemed quite powerful, but then she would go right back to the same behavior. Even though she kept saying, "Hey, he doesn't want me to approach him that way," she would still approach him in the same manner, and he would turn around and approach her with ears back. She didn't seem to be able to make the connection between her words and behaviors.

One day we were in session with her, and a hawk flew over. The hawk screeched, making us all look up, including the horses. She said, "Wow! I'm really connected to that hawk. I'd like to be like that hawk and have a bird's-eye view."

So she took a barrel and put it right up against the arena fence. She put a chair on top of this barrel, creating a perch she could then climb onto from the fence. Once perched up in the air, she said she had a bird's-eye view and could clearly see what was happening and what she needed to do. As soon as she said that, Fred came over and very matter-of-factly took his nose and pushed it against the barrel. The barrel fell out from under Jane, knocking her off and over the fence. She got up on the other side of the fence with Fred standing there on the inside.

We asked her about what just happened. She thought a minute and said, "I can say what I think I need to say, but somehow I can't seem to change my behavior. A lot of people believe what I say, but Fred is the first one to confront me when what I said did not match what I was doing. I made a pedestal, and Fred knocked me off my pedestal."

After Fred knocked her off her pedestal, she finally started to shift a bit, changing her movements toward the horses and slowing way down. She took her time. A few sessions later, we asked her, "Who is Fred?"

She said that for the first few sessions, she thought Fred was somebody she admired and liked, somebody she wanted to get. Over time Fred became who she wanted to *be*, a person who was congruent, who held her accountable to herself.

She was in therapy with us for an extended period of time. She disclosed that she had been seeing another therapist for eighteen years, who recently ended the therapeutic relationship because the therapist felt Jane was treatment resistant and not getting anywhere.

For the EAGALA Model, eight to nine months is a long time. It took her a long time to change, but finally we saw some profound things, specifically when she was able to walk with Fred—who now represented herself—beside her, shoulder to shoulder, without touching in any way. That was the day she announced she was going to turn in her license and stop practicing mental health altogether. "I'm much healthier now, but I can see I have too much other stuff going on to do this."

She was able to make decisions without being dependent on us or the horses and finally reached a point where she didn't feel the need to come back. We still saw her every now and then, when she came back to work with Fred or maybe another horse. She saw those sessions as getting "back in tune" with herself, to practice relationship skills.

It's been several years since we've heard from Jane, but she was doing well the last time we heard. She has a housecleaning business. She not only gave up her mental health license but decided not to go to any more dancing nights either. This client had quite a long progression of sessions compared to most of our clients. But thanks to Fred, she finally found her way.

Throughout this process, facilitators must always remember a key EAGALA principle: we are not there to change the client or the client's metaphor; we are there to explore the metaphor, so the client can begin understanding it. When this is accomplished successfully, within the client's story, change for the client occurs naturally.

Self-Distancing

In an EAGALA session, we use the client's physical, external experience with the horse to process his or her internal experiences, and through the SPUD'S process "hold up pictures" of moments from the experience for the client to reexamine. In EAGALA training, processing through this physical, external experience versus internal rumination becomes an important area of focus. The EAGALA Model uses a concept called self-distancing to bring attention to the horses and what happened in the arena, not the clients themselves.

The ability to self-distance in the retelling of a negative experience or story allows storytellers to retain some form of objectivity in how they see that story. A first-person retelling keeps the client-storytellers squarely in their old response patterns, so they reexperience both the mental and physical result. In contrast, the third person allows a different perspective, shifting the client-storyteller from "recounting/reliving" to reconstructing the story in a new way—a way that provides insight.[12]

In EAGALA, we talk about "processing through the horses." This means when we discuss the horse experiences with the clients, we focus on the horses and other symbols in the space and not on the clients themselves. So instead of saying, "There was a moment when you picked up a rope and put it on a horse," we instead say, "The rope went on a horse," or "The horse didn't have a rope on, and then did."

In the case of Jane above, she was able to shift her beliefs and behaviors around relationships through the horses. Ultimately, the horse became

12 Ethan Kross and Ozlem Ayduk, "Making Meaning out of Negative Experiences by Self-Distancing," *Current Directions in Psychological Science* 20 no. 3 (2011): 187–191.

a representation of the "self" she wanted to be, someone who could be congruent and accountable. She was able to work on herself through an outside, physical, live being she could touch and change, a being that was giving constant feedback. Through the process, the facilitators were able to focus not on Jane herself but the patterns and shifts that the horse, which represented Jane, was making. As the horse began changing, so did Jane naturally through the process.

In a solution-oriented model, we want facilitators to develop the ability to use physical moments and clean facilitation and language effectively, so the client can lead us to what's important to him or her. Clients create the visual picture and the metaphors. Facilitators learn not to put their interpretation on these pictures and metaphors, but to explore the client's response for more information.

Accept and Build: Using the Art of Improvisation

Once the metaphoric story begins, the next key skill set for facilitators is to support the flow of that story so that it builds and expands where the client and horses take it. This does not mean there are no goals, as we do work toward treatment and other identified goals. However, the EAGALA Model, in its true form, is facilitated in the present moment, relying completely on the horses and clients to inform the agenda. *The facilitators have no script.*

While trainees learn methods in the EAGALA fundamental trainings on how to build a progression of sessions and support the flow of the story, remaining truly in the moment and building off clients and horses is an advanced skill covered in depth during advanced trainings. These principles are supported through the art of improvisation.

Why improv? Most people associate improvisation with comedy and entertainment, something that only belongs in the realm of creative and gifted actors. In reality, improv involves specific techniques and training, and in the case of the EAGALA Model, training that can vastly improve our skills as facilitators.

Improvisational skills involve learning to respond to the client with a "yes, and" response. This form of allowing, through "yes, and" works by silencing the client's internal censor, helping the client build a linked chain of ideas so that a story can emerge. As the session progresses, this allows the client input to flow with ease. When clients learn to anticipate positive response and acceptance of their story, they become willing to offer more and more. Through these skilled techniques, the facilitators "play host" to clients, welcoming their story through "accepting and building." A story begins to form, and momentum grows.

In contrast, the opposite response of "accepting" and "yes, and" has a blocking effect. The improv concept of accepting keeps the client in control of the story, while blocking does the opposite. Facilitators learn to discern the many subtle ways blocking can occur, from the interference of their own Apostrophe S and need to get the "right answer" to the many ways their agenda can assert itself into the session.

Improvisation within sessions can take many forms, using deliberate and specific techniques to build the arc of the client's story. Most of the cases in this book utilize improvisation, where the facilitators went with the flow determined by the horses and clients in the moment. The story below gives another example of improvising and the "yes, and" principle.

This story is called "Have Car, Will Travel." The family in this case came to us through Community Services, wanting us to work with a young man, "Sam," who was diagnosed with high-functioning autism spectrum disorder. The day of the first session arrived, and they didn't show up and had not called to cancel. We called and learned they didn't keep the appointment because they literally couldn't get the client into the car!

We scheduled the session again, but Mom was skeptical. "If we *do* get him into the car, how are we going to get him out once we reach your place?" I thought about it for a second and then said, "I have an idea. If you can get him to the farm, just leave the rest to us."

The treatment team and I talked and created the plan. If they were able to get Sam to the farm and then out of the car, we were going to show him around the farm before inviting him into the arena. However, if they weren't able to get him out of the car, we were going to have them drive their car straight into the arena and see what happened next.

I notified the parents but advised them not to drive a nice car. "There's no telling what might happen," I said when I shared our backup plan.

The day arrived, and sure enough, the minute the parents pulled in and got out of the van, Sam stayed inside and immediately locked the doors behind them. "Don't worry. I've got the keys," said Dad.

"OK," I said, "then I need you to get back in the car and drive it into the arena, like we talked about. But before you get out, roll the windows down and open all the doors."

The parents got back in the car and drove into the arena, much to Sam's surprise. Mom and Dad got back out, leaving all the doors and windows wide open. As the parents walked out of the arena, we let the horses in. We chose my miniature horses, who are really curious, along with a couple of other horses who have high play drives.

Sam was in the car and noticed the horses. He started yelling, "What are you doing? Don't leave me in here!"

My MH and I looked at each other. We really were not sure how this was going to work. So we simply waited while Sam yelled and the parents watched. We didn't ask anything of the client; we just stood back.

We didn't have to wait long. Twister, one of my minis, lost no time getting into the action. He walked up to the van and just hopped right in, not even bothering to sniff it. The second he hopped in one side, Sam immediately hopped out the other. He stood in the arena, looking really surprised at first. The horses slowly proceeded to come over and check him out.

At the moment he connected with the horses, it felt very important to continue standing back. We dropped our planned activities and didn't engage him further, verbally or otherwise, for the rest of that first session. Each moment happening was not planned or predictable. We had to go with the flow and see where the horses and client continued to take it.

Watching, Mom and Dad were pretty darn happy; the fact that Sam wasn't creating havoc, even for just a moment, was a shift for them. This little bit of change was a huge release, something they didn't get to see from him a whole lot.

He came for several more sessions, and each session required us to stay in the moment and see where Sam would take it next. Dad just kept driving the car into the arena, and by the third time, when Mom and Dad got out of the van, Sam jumped out on his own. The fourth time, we had the parents park outside the arena to see what happened. Sure enough, Sam got out and walked straight into the arena. By the fifth session, he was excited to come and even got into the car by himself before leaving home.

While Sam's behavior was showing changes, the horses were showing Unique Shifts as well. In particular, Twister hung out with this client a lot. He's normally a horse that really pushes buttons and agitates people, but he was always calm and constant with Sam. It was interesting, as Twister was the horse that created that first "Shift" in Sam by jumping in the van and after that continued to be the one Sam connected with the most and seemed to have the most changes in his behavior.

From the word *go*, this was a client who was treatment resistant. The parents had not been able to get him to do anything on a voluntary basis; everything was by force. Over time we were able to see him go from refusing to get in the car to being eager to come to the barn. Eventually he started having real conversations with the horses and then started having real conversations with us. But the process—and improvisation—were the key every step of the way.

It isn't easy to be in this place of following the client's and horses' story, of accepting it versus blocking it. Our Apostrophe S wants to direct the process and make sure something happens. Especially in the case above, the facilitators could have fallen into the role of forcing the client, just like his parents had. The Shift occurred when they used "yes, and" with the client. The client chose to be in the van, and so the facilitators did not block that choice. Instead they imparted a message that it was OK to be in the van and simply moved the van into the arena. From there, the facilitators were able to watch a story unfold while *the horses did the work of creating shifts.* Perhaps Twister wouldn't have jumped in the van. Perhaps the client would have stayed inside. None of that matters because the facilitators used what happened and went with the flow.

It is not uncommon for some clients to display reluctance to go into the arena. Whether for fear or other reasons, this reluctance becomes part of their metaphor. It is OK to stay on this side of the gate, because *this side, gate,* and *the other side* all become powerful symbols—characters in the client's story.

While facilitators can influence the story by creating a space where insights and shifts can occur, we need to be careful we're not directing what we *think* needs to happen and how quickly it should happen. The power of the EAGALA Model comes from allowing the horses to create the shifts.

This in turn allows us as facilitators to be with the clients in whatever place they are in.

Applying the Skills

The stories above provide more examples of how each client experience can be unique. No two stories are ever alike. The individual dynamics of each case determine how the client story will flow. The advanced skills of EAGALA practitioners allow clients more tools to access the full potential of change horses can evoke in each therapeutic context. The development of high-level facilitation skills gives practitioners the ability to set the stage and open doors with greater effectiveness and consistency.

Facilitators who use these skills to create and hold this space—with curiosity and moment-by-moment presence, session after session—are the ones who become most successful in facilitating the clients' movement through their story to their own solution.

PART IV

Conclusion

CHAPTER 9

Putting It Together

There are numerous stories of how clients learn to take their EAGALA experience into their world outside the session. One young man comes to mind from my cases, one who is currently in prison with a life term as a habitual felon. I once asked him if there was anything about the time he spent working with the horses in his treatment that was still with him today. I wanted to know if it made a difference and how often he used what he learned.

"Every day," was his reply. "I use what I learned about horses and herds every day. Treating this environment as a herd has taught me how to survive here. I understand the herd mentality, how to assess who is dominant and who is submissive. I know when it's comfortable to be in the herd and when to shift into flight mentality. When the herd gets into fight mode, I know it's safer for me to move...and I'm usually the only one moving."

This young man was in treatment ten years ago, and he is still using what he learned. He took what he needed to take from the process, and now it helps him survive in the environment he's in.

When performed at the highest level, EAGALA Model facilitation allows the full potential of the process—the power of horses, the belief in the client, and the skills of the facilitators—to happen so that positive change can take place. The components of the

EAGALA Model help us to create an ideal environment for exploration, problem solving, and discovery.

For those who are open and aware, the horse-human interaction never loses its ability to both humble and surprise us, no matter our years of experience or how extensive our educational degrees and honors. The cases illustrated in this book—whether funny or sad or profound—are but a small sample of EAGALA's tremendous capacity to result in deep and powerful results.

In the EAGALA Model, our client interactions often look very different from what we anticipate. Sometimes entire sessions happen with little visible movement or discussion. Sometimes there appears to be no visible progress at all. Yet over and over again, we see how profound internal shifts can happen with little outward evidence, shifts that may not even register in our awareness until down the road in the client's treatment. The influence of the experiential component goes beyond intellectual change to imprint learning and growth onto the body itself. Like a muscle memory, solutions manifest mentally, emotionally, and physically.

Throughout the stories in this book, the receptivity and willingness of the facilitators to learn continually is a key component for success. As we've seen, you cannot operate within this model of facilitation while also having an ego or directing the process, lest you find yourself being humbled again and again by the horse. The professionalism and standards of EAGALA facilitators make all the difference.

In the end, it's these skills that help us set the stage. What happens between the horse and client is beyond our control. Our job is to hold the space so the horses can do what they do best and clients can discover their own meaning.

A lot of people want to know just how the EAGALA Model works. They also want to know if it's really effective. When we're promoting it and talking about it, it's hard to describe. Pure and simple, it's just something you need to experience. This story may describe it best. It's one client's explanation of why the EAGALA Model worked for him when all other modalities failed. I call this case "It's Like This, Mister."

This story began when we started working with a client who had been in out-of-home placement since the age of eight. He had been everywhere: in different youth wilderness camps, ranch environments, detention, you name it—a real mixed bag of very structured settings. He had failed most of them, meaning he was either removed from the program or did not complete the objectives, so he was sent to the next program.

He was fifteen when he came to us, living in residential treatment and coming out with a group to work with the horses. In a short period of time, this client really started to excel. He did everything he could possibly do to be able to come to the barn for sessions. We saw how well he was working the program, being extremely thorough and making progress fairly quickly.

We kept sending updates to his probation officer and his containment team. After he was with us for three or four months, the probation officer of his containment team finally stepped forward and said, "I've known this kid a long time, and I know he's pulling one over on you. He can't be doing this good. He's flunked out of everything. I can't believe there's really anything different about your program."

We invited him to come to the barn and check it out, but he resisted, saying, "I just want to get to the bottom of this. I want to confront Steven." We managed to convince him to come to the barn first and watch the Friday session.

When the probation officer showed up, we were already in the middle of Steven's session. He was in the round pen working with a two-year-old Arabian colt.

The probation officer leaned on the fence and watched. Finally, he called out, "Steven, what are you doing, pulling something over on these people? When are you going to start showing your true colors?"

My MH and I winced to hear those words coming from this guy. I'll never forget what happened next.

Steven just stopped what he was doing, looked his probation officer in the eye with hands on his hips, and said, "Well, mister, it's like this: When I'm sitting in a four-walled office and I put my stuff out there, it just bounces off the wall and jumps right back on me. But out here, when I give it to the horses, they do something with it. It's not mine anymore. *That's* what's different about this." Then he went back to working with his horse.

The probation officer stood there for a moment and then looked at us and just said, "Well." He thanked us for our time, got in his car, and left. There wasn't much more to say.

This probation officer never expressed any negativity again. Steven continued to excel through the program and do some really great work with the horses. That was several years ago. He went on to be an upstanding young man in the community. He went into the military and has a family of his own now.

Steven's feedback was a pivotal piece of information for me too. It was an interesting piece of insight that, in his eyes, the horses "did something with his stuff."

When I was a kid, my uncle Earl always told me, "You know, Mark, horses can smell fear, so you don't need to let them know you're scared." I think back on that as a kid, working and hanging around my uncle and his horses. I think it's more than just smelling fear; I think that horses can read our intentions; they're able to read us like a book. I truly believe that if given the opportunity to let the horses be themselves, they will never fail to meet people at the right point.

Our job here is complete if we succeed in helping each reader walk away understanding the importance of sustaining the key EAGALA principles, along with a perpetual mind-set of curiosity, humility, and acceptance of the unknown and unexplainable.

The EAGALA Model is simple and yet not simple. It's not without irony that it is the practitioners, not the horses, who need training. The practitioner is the one who must learn to let go, get out of the way, and allow the opportunities for healing and change to occur. When the practitioner embraces this reality and engages his or her development of skill sets in the model, the result is a truly potent combination to transform lives: client, horse, and the equine specialists and mental health professionals that make up the EAGALA team.

Tribute to Mon-Jour (and all the horses healing lives through EAGALA)
by Mark Lytle

Early on we decided to dedicate this book to all the EAGALA therapy horses out there, the horses that make these changes and shifts possible in people's lives.

We all have that one horse, the one horse that gets deepest into our hearts, and the one that does the most amazing things with people. The one that is the hardest good-bye.

Mon-Jour was that horse for me and more. Many things about him were remarkable: the fact that he lived to the extraordinary age of thirty-two; the fact that I was nine years old when he entered my life, and that he stayed with me from childhood through high school, college, two marriages, the death of my mother, and the birth of my three kids.

No doubt about it, Mon-Jour was a powerful force for me, from childhood until his passing in 2012. I've been given the task of recording and sharing his story, and I've really struggled to put the words down, remembering how much he gave to me and to many other people over the years. Missing him now more than ever, I realize I still grieve for him today.

Horsemen will tell you "green on green makes black and blue." It was true: a nine-year-old green kid and a green horse made for some very interesting situations in Mon-Jour's early years. But it also created a foundation that was absolutely unbreakable. I have story upon story about how he did things, first during my horse-training years and then in my EAGALA years. I showed Mon-Jour as a kid and gave riding lessons on him as an adult, where he taught numerous people how to ride. We rode him in horse shows and on the trail.

But it's the fact that he was one of the most remarkable horses I ever worked with in my whole career that really stands out to me, both as a horse trainer and as an EAGALA equine specialist.

This story is called "Weathering the Storm." A five-year-old client named "Mary" and her seven-year-old brother, "Ben," were referred to us. They were in therapeutic foster care in separate homes, and the caseworker wanted to use EAGALA sessions to help reintegrate them into a single home. Grandmother had relinquished custody to the Department of Social Services.

The van from the group home arrived, and when Mary got out, my heart just kind of melted. Here she was, a beautiful child with blond hair in ponytails and big blue eyes. I thought this was going to be the sweetest session, reuniting these two kids.

We went into the arena. Mary was very excited to be there. Ben was quiet and reserved. We asked them to introduce themselves to the horses, a big Clydesdale, a Haflinger, a miniature horse, and Mon-Jour.

It didn't take long for things to start happening. After a few moments, Mary went running and screaming up to the Clydesdale. He jumped about two inches off the ground, wheeled around in surprise, and looked at her with wide eyes. She moved toward him again, and he moved quickly out of her way. This only made her more animated. She started yelling and screaming at top volume, and in no time, the Clydesdale, the Haflinger, and the mini were running around the arena. It sounded like thunder as they went—*vroom, vroom.* Dust was flying. The MH and I found ourselves, with the brother, plastered up against the wall of the arena.

This didn't go over too well with Mary. She took her shoes off and threw them at the horses. Her face got bright red and looked positively distorted, as if she were possessed. She didn't even look like the same child, screaming and swearing at the top of her lungs, using language no five-year-old should even know.

The horses continued to run in circles until all of a sudden, the Clydesdale decided he'd had enough. He ran straight at the wood fence at the back of the arena, pushed into it, and broke through. As he left, he took the mini and Haflinger with him. We were still backed up against the arena wall. I looked out and saw various family members in the distance, dropping whatever they were doing on the farm to go after the horses. I knew the horses would be OK.

At the same time, I was rather shocked. I looked at my MH partner and said, "What should we do here?"

My MH said, "Let's just keep watching and see what happens." So we turned back to the arena.

Mary spent the next twenty minutes screaming and cussing, becoming even angrier now that the horses had left. She was barefoot, and her ponytails were completely messed up. Mary's voice and body language got more and more animated as she went into a full-blown tantrum.

It was then I realized Mon-Jour, my old Arabian gelding, was still in the arena—but he didn't look happy. His body faced the back gate, legs spread wide apart, chin low, and tail clamped. He looked exactly like a horse weathering a storm.

Mary went on screaming without letup. Then Mon-Jour reached a point where he'd had enough. He seemed to square up, as if making a decision. He turned around, walked up to the child, and grabbed a hold of her ponytail with his mouth. He then literally walked her over to us, pulling her ponytail so she had to come with him.

When they reached us, Mon-Jour opened up his mouth, put his lips on her forehead, and stretched his neck so he was holding her at the very end of his reach. If you've ever seen someone put a hand on someone's forehead, with an arm outstretched, so the other person is unable to reach to hit or make contact, that is exactly what this looked like. Mon-Jour was keeping her firmly at arm's length. Mary didn't know what to do; she could scream and swing all she wanted, but she wasn't going anywhere.

Big brother chose this moment to chime in: "This is just like Christmas!"

We looked at each other, thinking the same thing: *That must have been some Christmas!*

We also realized that was quite a statement coming from a seven-year-old, to look at this situation and make that kind of comment. As the session ended, Mary was still being held at bay by Mon-Jour. When it was time to go, he simply moved away and walked off. At this point, Mary was out of steam and followed the case worker and foster parents to the van and left.

After the session, we learned the siblings had come from a domestic-violence situation, where they witnessed the mother killing their father. Grandma took custody of the children after this, but Mary was very reactive and would throw these tantrums over just about anything.

As to the brother's comment, we learned that during the previous Christmas, the extended family members arrived at Grandma's house for dinner and presents on Christmas Day. When Mary wanted to do the presents first, Grandma said no, and Mary reacted by throwing the epitome of all tantrums. She threw the dinner turkey across the room, pushed over the Christmas tree, and started breaking things—screaming and swearing the entire time. Amid the chaos, the family members left. The next morning, Grandma packed up the kids' bags and took them to the Department of Social Services, saying, "Here, I'm done."

The brother, at seven, was able to look at the experience in the arena and make the connection to that Christmas experience and how it led to them being placed in foster care.

After that first session, we honestly didn't think they would come back. However, they showed up the next week, and the caseworker said, "I don't know what you did last week; just do it again."

The surprise must have shown on our faces. "Really? Do it again?"

The caseworker explained that when Mary returned to her foster-care home, she was able to do her homework, eat dinner, and get ready for bed without being physically restrained—the first time this child did not have to be physically restrained in the home. The caseworker and foster parents knew something had shifted, and it was enough of a change that they wanted Mary to come back. It appeared Mon-Jour's "intervention" had done its work at some level. He broke through to that little girl in a way no one else could.

During the second session, we once again invited the kids to introduce themselves to the horses. This time, Mary moved a little slower, and the session went much better. Things wrapped up without incident. As sessions progressed week by week, Mary had her ups and downs and would still throw the occasional tantrum. But as treatment progressed, Mary's behavior continued to improve, to the point where she went full days without physical restraint, and then a few days, and then a week, and then to almost none. She ultimately got adopted by a family and became very involved in working with horses, doing very well behaviorally and in school.

As an EAGALA horse, Mon-Jour logged about five thousand hours of these therapy sessions. He handled everything, calling people on their stuff, testing boundaries, and correcting bad behavior. Anytime there was a secret to be disclosed, Mon-Jour was up to the task, including pulling the wig off a cancer patient who hadn't told anyone of her diagnosis. He was even EAGALA Therapy Horse of the Year. He ended up being the topic of many of my stories, with an expressive and curious personality that made him seem much bigger than his 14.3 hands.

As the years ticked by, I eventually noticed he was moving a little slower. When the younger horses were roughhousing, he couldn't move out of the way as fast as he once could. So we built a paddock up in front of my dad's house for him.

On the day Mon-Jour passed, he was thirty-two years old. My daughter was taking him up to his paddock, and the therapist and I were in the middle of a session. We heard this blood-curdling scream from my daughter. "Dad!" Then I heard my dad holler for me. When I reached the paddock, Mon-Jour was already on the ground.

He tried to get up three times. When he looked at me that third time, I just knew he was gone. I knew what I needed to do for him, because he *never* had a problem doing what he needed to do for me or anybody else. I made the call to have him put down.

My vet was out of town. I called my backup vet, and he was going to be delayed several hours on another case. I had no option but to call a third vet, a vet I'd rarely spoken to since we had parted ways on bad terms twenty years earlier. I reached her receptionist and said, "Tell her that this is Mark Lytle and that Mon-Jour is down. I need her now." The vet pulled up to the farm fifteen minutes later.

Mon-Jour was with me for about forty-five minutes. I was able to lie with him and tell him good-bye. All of our current therapists and everybody else on our team came to say good-bye as well. There was an outpouring of love and support in that moment that I've never forgotten. To think that a horse, just a plain old horse, could bring people together like he did that day is the very reason I still get so emotional even just talking about him.

When I look back now, I realize that even in his last moments, Mon-Jour was still influencing people. When the vet arrived, our differences were forgotten. He brought us back together and helped us mend our friendship.

This is the story of just one horse. The power of Mon-Jour—and all the other therapy horses out here in the world—is that, when given the space, the time, and the opportunity, they are better for people than almost anything else I know.

I can't think of many pathways more respectful to horses than the work we do in EAGALA, truly allowing horses to take care of themselves and others in a way that we as facilitators, therapists, and horse people will never fully understand. It's just amazing. Is it magic? Is it science? Is it pheromones that they read and smell? I'm not sure we'll ever know, but I'm going to keep walking this path.

I still see pieces of Mon-Jour show up every day in other horses, both those I know and those I've just met. All horses have it. The only regret I have is taking so long to realize the talent these great creatures have. If only I had recognized and harnessed that when I was nine, ten, and twelve years old, what a blessing that would've been.

With this, I say thank you to Mon-Jour, to all the other therapy horses I've known, and to the ones I'll never even meet. They're out there every day, doing their work without getting much in return. I hope everyone comes to recognize how these horses grace our lives.

References

Avolio, Beth. "Strategies to Resist the Assist." *EAGALA in Practice*, 4 no. 1 (2011): 22–23.

EAGALA. *Fundamentals of the EAGALA Model, 8th Edition Training Manual.* Santaquin, UT: EAGALA, 2015.

Kelleher, Margaret. "Still Points: Letting the Horse Be the Therapist." *EAGALA in Practice*, 4 no. 1 (2011): 38–39.

Kross, Ethan, and Ozlem Ayduk. "Making Meaning Out of Negative Experiences by Self-Distancing." *Current Directions in Psychological Science*, 20 no. 3 (2011): 187–191.

Lawley, James, and Penny Tompkins. *Metaphors in Mind: Transformation through Symbolic Modelling.* London: The Developing Company Press, 2000.

"National Welfare Code of Practice," American Horse Council, accessed February 21, 2016, http://www.horsecouncil.org/national-welfare-code.

Index of Stories

For more information on EAGALA, the Equine Assisted Growth and Learning Association, visit eagala.org or call 1-877-858-4600 to

- find EAGALA Model services near you;
- support this powerful work with horses changing lives through your donations and sponsorships;
- become an EAGALA Certified Professional;
- obtain educational materials for academic coursework.

Made in the USA
Columbia, SC
12 May 2018